BEYOND QUESTIONS AND ANSWERS

BEYOND QUESTIONS AND ANSWERS

The Creed for Today's Catholic

TIMOTHY S. McDERMOTT

BURNS & OATES / HERDER AND HERDER

BURNS & OATES LIMITED
25 Ashley Place, London S.W.1.
First publication in Great Britain, 1968

Reproduced and printed in Great Britain by
Billing & Sons Limited, Guildford and London

CONTENTS

5

CONTENTS

7

A*

For Anne

BEYOND QUESTIONS AND ANSWERS

PRELIMINARIES

Who made you?
God made me.

This exchange seems quite simple and true. Well, it is true, but is it so simple? Think what chaos might have been introduced into the catechism class if some bright child had asked, "And who is God?" For what answer could there have been but "God is the person who made me"? If we substitute this definition of God in our original catechism question and answer, we get the following exchange: *Who made you? The person who made me made me.* Now this is quite true, but it does not seem very enlightening.

If one asked a refrigerator who made it, one might get the answer, "General Electric made me"; and then if one asked, "And who is General Electric?", it would at least be possible to describe General Electric and give its history and say where its main offices are to be found. But who can describe God, or give his history, or locate his main offices? When we ask who God is we pretty soon get into a vicious circle.

Now all this does not make the catechism untrue, but it does show that it is not quite so enlightening as it seems to be on the face of it. There is no getting around the fact that men do not know much about God: not because there is nothing to know, but because there is too much to know and our minds are very small. Whenever we try to describe God we must use words taken from our limited world: words such as *person* and *good* and *holy,* and even *father* and *son* and *spirit.* We have some idea of what these words mean in our world, but who has any real idea of what they mean in God? We are in the rather odd posi-

19

tion of knowing that they are true, without quite knowing what they mean.

All this is of the greatest importance in the project we have set ourselves. It shows us that God really is a mystery which men will never get to the bottom of. Even when we know truth about God, and know it without a doubt, we can still be very unsure as to its meaning. We must never think that we—even we in the Church—are thoroughly acquainted with God and cannot learn anything new about him. We must always be open to fresh light, from wherever it comes. We must be prepared to listen to any man who is sincerely grappling with the mystery of God. We cannot afford to say, "We know all about that already."

On the other hand, what we learn must be in tune with what we already know. New glimpses of truth must be in continuity with old glimpses. This is so especially because the Christian has the guarantee of a true tradition.

As Christians we have been given a gift for which we cannot be too grateful: we have been given another possible answer to the bright child's question, "And who is God?" We can answer this question by saying, "God is the person revealed to us in Jesus Christ." Now we *can* go on to give some sort of description of Jesus Christ, to recount his history and tell men where he can be found. There is indeed a certain sense in which God's main offices have a very earthly address.

But this is the only special knowledge about God that Christians have. To know God means, therefore, to know more and more about the man Jesus Christ who was God, and to know more and more about his Father and his Spirit. The tradition by which we judge everything is the tradition about Jesus handed down through his Spirit from the very first beginnings of the Christian Church. It is this tradition which is enshrined in the Apostles' Creed and which we shall be considering in this book.

THE PURPOSE OF MAN

Why did God make you?

God made me to know him, love him, and serve him in this
world, and to be happy with him forever in the next.

If we ask, "Why did General Electric make this refrigerator?"
we could be asking the *motive* for which they made it, or the
purpose for which it was made. If we are asking about General
Electric's motive the crude answer might be: To make money.
But if we are asking the purpose for which they made the refrigerator, the answer would then be: To keep food fresh. When
the catechism asks, "Why did God make you?" it might be asking for his motives (What did he get out of it?) or for his purposes (What purpose does his creation serve?).

The answer does not give God's motives, for it was not in
order to get our knowledge, love, and service for himself that he
made us; he is totally and infinitely complete already and has no
need of us. It is not to give *himself* anything that he has made
us, but to give *us* something. He wanted to give us first the gift
of ourselves, and then add the gift of himself as one of ourselves.
Indeed, we might say that God's *motive* in creating was that he
might know, love, and serve us in this world, and be happy with
us forever in the next.

But the catechism answer gives not God's motives but his purposes. It tells us what purpose we were meant to serve. Now the
purpose of man is, first of all, to accept the gift God is giving

21

him. Man alone can do this; no other creature has the freedom to say yes or no to God's purposes. Only in man is acceptance of God's purposes a matter of free choice, a task to be accomplished throughout life. That is why modern writers often define man as a being who is concerned with his own existence, a creature who must win himself. That is why you can exhort a man to *be* a man. You cannot exhort a crocodile to be a crocodile.

So we may say that mankind's purpose is to accept mankind, that is, to know, love, and serve the existence of mankind. Why then does the catechism say "to know, love, and serve God"? The answer is that these are not alternatives. To know, love, and serve man is to accept the gift that God has given, and thus to know, love, and serve the purposes of the giver. We cannot give anything to God; but we can know, love, and serve him by cooperating with his gift to man. So we often find modern Christians stressing that the service of mankind is the service of God. Did not St. John say, "No one can love God and hate his brother. No one has ever seen God, but if we love our brothers we have God dwelling in us."

But let us go on to the last catechism phrase: "to be happy with God forever in the next world." Why not in *this* world? Is it God's purpose that we should just work hard in this world without relief—knowing, loving, and serving creation—and then be suddenly transferred at death into quite a different kind of existence where everything is relief and there is no more work? Are this world and the next related like the office where we work to earn wages and home where we spend them? No. This world and the next are more closely related than that: not so much like office-work and wages, but like work in a garden and joy in the plants that grow there, like work on a farm and joy in the harvest.

22

Heaven comes not so much like wages from on high, but like a harvest slowly maturing within our lives here below. Heaven begins on earth. In our knowledge and love and service of men, and of God through men, we are building the community of men and God, the communion of saints, which is heaven. Moment by moment, as past gives way to present and present to future, we are preparing the harvest; but God is eternally present to that harvest and sees the place of every moment of history in it. What we hope for is to join him in that eternal presence and eternal joy.

We can now see how to rephrase the catechism answer without sacrificing its truth, but making it clearer to modern man. To the question "Why did God make you?" we answer, "God made me to know, love, and serve men in history, and God in men, and so to come to share that eternal joyous presence to the whole of history which belongs to God."

THE DIGNITY OF MAN

To whose image and likeness did God make you?
God made me to his own image and likeness.

In the modern world there is a great deal of talk about the dignity of the human person. The penny catechism summarizes the Christian view of man's dignity and worth in the single scriptural phrase, "made in God's image and likeness."

The phrase, first of all, includes all that the modern world wishes to say about the dignity of man. Man alone of material beings is free. That is to say, he can determine his own actions. Other things, even animals, are more acted upon—by their own instincts and nature—than acting; only man engages in action for which he and he alone is responsible. On the stage of this world, in the drama of history, everything else is so much stage-property; but man is a performer.

More than this, man is not only an actor, but he produces the play. He does not simply obey directions from on high as to how he is to act; he also directs himself, reflecting with intelligence upon the nature of the world and of the society in which he lives, and then playing his part with free will in the way which seems to him appropriate. Indeed, man not only produces and acts in the play, but he writes it. God's plot for the world is a developing plot, a plot which he calls on men to develop for him. God is writing his plot for the world now through each man's free actions; he is allowing man to write the plot for him and determine the way in which the world is going to go.

This freedom of man, which for the modern world is man's supreme dignity, is also an article of our faith. "God created man in the beginning," says the book of Ecclesiasticus, "and left him in the power of his own counsel." And the Psalmist exclaims, "You have made man little less than a god; with glory and honor you crowned him, gave him power over the works of your hand, put all things under his feet."

But sometimes the modern world wants to go further, and say that man's freedom must also involve being free from God. For notions such as God and heaven and life after death seem to many people to distract man from really being man, from really giving himself freely to his part here and now in the world drama. Belief in God, they say, encourages a man in nostalgia: that sickness of present life and "desire to be absent" which is the greatest infidelity to man's dignity that there can possibly be. Believers, many feel, behave in this world like lovesick and homesick people; they are inhibited and not fully free.

Even here the scripture to some extent agrees. For by making *man* in his own image God repudiated all those idolatrous images of God that men make for themselves. God has divorced himself from all that men have thought up in the way of gods. He will have no other image of himself in this world than free, responsible men. God, therefore, does not wish to distract man away from his call to freedom and responsibility; he wishes to appear most vividly, to be imaged most clearly, in man's freedom and responsibility.

Here one could reflect that there are two different kinds of images: those like statues and photographs that represent some absent person; and those like images in a mirror that represent a person only when he is present, and go away when the person goes away. Man is not a statue or a photograph of God; he is more like an image in a mirror, an image *in* which God is present, *in* which God is acting. The very dignity of man's freedom is a living reflection of the majesty of God making him free.

Finally, precisely because man has this dignity of freedom, he is able to converse with God. He can, so to speak, answer back when God questions. He can even question and have God answer back. This conversation with God, foreshadowed in the Old Testament in figures like Job, was brought to perfection in Jesus Christ, related to God as son to father, the true mirror image of God. Now this perfection of dignity is open to all men, who in Christ are not only responsible servants but have become friends of God, sons with Christ, living images of their Father.

MAN'S MAKE-UP

Is your likeness to God in your body or in your soul?

This likeness to God is chiefly in my soul.

How is your soul like to God?

My soul is like to God because it is a spirit and is immortal.

What do you mean when you say that your soul is immortal?

When I say that my soul is immortal I mean that my soul can never die.

The catechism has already spoken of the purpose of man and the dignity of man; in these three questions it speaks of his make-up. Men, it says, are unities of body and soul, where "soul" means undying spirit. But we shall surely misunderstand this definition unless we remember that in the biblical languages, Hebrew and Greek, "spirit" means "breath." Men are not spirits but have spirit in them; just as animals are not breaths but have breath in them.

If we were asked to distinguish animals from lower kinds of being we might answer that though all things are bodies of a sort, only animals are breathing bodies, only animals have breath in them. If we were asked to distinguish men from animals we might go on to say that men are animals with a *new* kind of breath in them, with "spirit" in them. This at least is how the Hebrews and Greeks put it.

A man, in other words, has another life in him deepening his bodily life. An animal's life is simply the life of its body, and at death when its bodily breath evaporates into the air it is finished. But a man's life is not simply the life *of* his body, though it is life *in* a body; and though his bodily breath may evaporate, another deeper "breath" remains.

This "breath" or "spirit" is only something that belongs to a man, it is not the man himself. "Spirit" is a part of man and not the whole of him; the whole man is body-and-spirit. So we must not think of ourselves simply as "spirits" unfortunately tied to our bodies during this life, but at death joyfully gaining our freedom. We are body-and-spirit, and death is a terrible tragedy which tears us apart.

Death does not annihilate us as it does animals, but it deeply and horribly wounds us. Our spirit may live on but our whole self does not, which is why pre-Christian civilizations spontaneously thought of the after-life as a ghost-life, a mere shadow of life.

But the Christian believes that he has *yet another life again* within his spirit, another "breath" again within his soul; and this other "breath" is nothing less than the "breath" of God, the Holy Spirit. This is the Spirit that Christ breathed into the world on Calvary, and which was breathed into us at baptism. And it is really *this* Spirit, even more than the soul, which makes us like to God.

For we are like to God because of our undying spirit, says the catechism. But our human spirit is undying only in the sense that death does not annihilate us. Death nevertheless horribly wounds us and reduces us to a ghost of our former self. The divine Spirit of Christ is undying in a much greater sense. For this Spirit actually thrives on death. Or rather, it is just precisely at the moment of death that it can realize itself most perfectly;

for it is the Spirit of God himself, and God is love, and greater love no man has than that he lay down his life for his friends.

When Christ died, his innermost life of the Spirit really came to fulfillment, and with such power that his body even was raised again to a new life. And so it will be with us. The undying Spirit of God is breathing in us; our death will bring to fulfillment his life in us; and at the resurrection the wound of death will be made whole and we shall live, body-and-soul, with God's life for ever.

These thoughts can help us better to understand the catechism answers. The catechism does not say that we are souls, but that we are unities of body-and-soul. It does not teach that our souls are undying spirits in the same sense that God is an undying spirit, only that there is a kind of resemblance. But there is not enough resemblance to give us any sort of worthwhile life of our own after death. The only worthwhile life after death is God's life, and we can share it only if God injects his own undying spirit into us. Our Christian hope lies not in having an immortal soul, but in having Christ's spirit of total love in our hearts.

Nor does the catechism say that our likeness to God is *only* in our soul. Just as life in animals makes their bodies into something quite different from inanimate bodies, so does the human spirit make a human body something quite different from an animal body. Human faces and lips and hands are themselves vivid expressions of our human intelligence and freedom. Christian faces should be something more again: living expressions of Christian love and therefore the most shining images and likenesses of God.

29

MAN'S TASK

Of which must you take most care, your body or your soul?

I must take most care of my soul; for Christ has said, "What does it profit a man if he gain the whole world and suffer the loss of his own soul?"

What must you do to save your soul?

To save my soul I must worship God by faith, hope, and charity; that is, I must believe in him, I must hope in him, and I must love him with my whole heart.

These are two of the most puzzling and distressing answers in the catechism. They are distressing because of their tone, which seems to many people selfish. I am exhorted apparently to *use* friendship with God as a means to my own health of soul. This is like being exhorted to use walks with a friend simply as a means to my own health of body.

Again, these are puzzling answers. The catechism has just defined the soul as an undying spirit. What then can it mean: to lose my soul? The soul would seem to be the one thing I cannot lose. One can see some point in trying to preserve the health of the body which can die, but if the soul is undying, will it not preserve itself?

Here let us remember that the soul is an undying spirit only in the sense that death does not annihilate me. Nevertheless, death wounds me horribly and reduces me to a ghost of my former self, so that to live on after death as just a soul would not in itself be a worthwhile life. The only worthwhile life after death is God's life, and we can share this life only if God injects *his* undying spirit, his Holy Spirit, into us.

There are thus two ways of preserving life in ourselves. One is the preserving of this present life, which requires care of the body. The other is God's eternal life in us, which requires, not so much care of the soul, as care of the undying spirit of love for men which Christ has breathed into us, body-and-soul, from Calvary. The first catechism answer above is talking about these two ways of preserving life, though in slightly puzzling language. It is telling us that, though we must care both for the body and for God's life within us, we must care "most" for the second, because it is a deeper life and more fruitful.

Now we can see that my life with God is important not only because it is *my* life and will give *me* happiness—by itself this could be thought selfish—but also because it is *his* life, the life he has chosen to lead with me, and gives *him* happiness, again because it is a life of love for men, and will bring *them* happiness. One must get away from the tone that suggests we are engaged on a program of health and beauty for our souls, a business project in which we strike up friendship with God for planned returns. Caring for the body will preserve only my individual life, but caring for one's life with God is like caring for one's married life, it is caring for the life of others as well.

If, in fact, we asked a husband and wife how they were to care for their married life, each might say: My married life depends on my worshipping my partner by faith, hope, and charity; to preserve our marriage I must believe my wife or husband, trust him or her, and love him or her with my whole heart. In certain marriage services each partner says to the other,

31

"With my body I thee worship." That is, each puts himself or herself totally at the service of the other, gives himself or herself to a married life with his or her partner. Our life with God is like this life of wife and husband, totally given in sacrifice.

Since giving is the expression of love, and love is only truly possible on a basis of trust, and trust involves being able to believe one's partner, so also our life with God is a life of belief, trust, and love.

Never let us forget this personal character of life with God. To regard prayer, for example, solely as some planned step in a project of saving one's soul, is like regarding conversation with someone whom one loves as merely a move to trap him or her into marriage and thus gain security for oneself. We are often in danger of trying to "seduce" God and use him for our purposes.

Life with God is a spontaneous love affair in which we seek and delight in his company, finding it of course mainly in his presence in other men and women. So we might rephrase the catechism answer thus: "Our life depends on loving our fellow men, and thus expressing our belief in, trust in, and love of Christ on Calvary. It was there that God showed love for us, and in response we love the brethren."

So we are not to go through life thinking only of keeping our soul free from stain, like somebody running an egg-and-spoon race tries to keep his egg from falling off his spoon. If the soul is an egg, it is one to be sat upon and hatched; made fruitful for others, not simply saved for oneself.

We are called then to a life of love for God and men; and like any other love-life, it demands belief and trust in the person we love. Belief, trust, and love of God we call faith, hope, and charity; and the catechism now discusses each of these in turn. In this book we deal only with faith.

32

INTRODUCTION TO
THE APOSTLES' CREED

What is faith?
Faith is a supernatural gift of God which enables us to believe without doubting whatever God has revealed.

Why must you believe whatever God has revealed?
I must believe whatever God has revealed because God is the very truth and can neither deceive nor be deceived.

How are you to know what God has revealed?
I am to know what God has revealed by the testimony, teaching and authority of the Catholic Church.

Who gave the Catholic Church divine authority to teach?
Jesus Christ gave the Catholic Church divine authority to teach when he said, "Go and teach all nations."

The catechism is saying that for the Catholic, belief in God expresses itself in belief in Jesus Christ, and belief in Jesus Christ expresses itself in belief in the Catholic Church. Moreover, our faith is said to be a response to God's *revelation* and to the Church's *testimony, teaching,* and *authority:* four words for us to ponder.

Revelation. We tend to think of faith rather narrowly as blind assent to certain dogmas. But does not this word suggest something wider? It means "unveiling," and it usually refers to some *happening* that unveils the truth for us, rather than to some statement of truth. Thus if we are vouchsafed an unexpected glimpse of the way the poor live, we may call it an "absolute revelation" and feel we have learned more than from any number of lectures. Even when we refer to a man's conversation as "very revealing" we often think less of what he said than of the way he said it, and sometimes indeed we think precisely of what he did *not* say. People "reveal" their friendship for us less by what they say than by what they do: "Actions speak louder than words."

So also with God. His revelation is his revealing himself to be our friend, and this he has done less by words than by his actions in history. Faith is our response to that revelation, our accepting of his proffered friendship as *true* friendship. Our faith also expresses itself less in our words than in our actions of relying on God's friendship: acts of faith in God, as we call them.

Testimony. This helps us to understand the word *testimony* or *witness* better. A witness is someone who retails incidents to us which we have not seen for ourselves. Nobody has ever seen God, but we have Jesus Christ as a witness, someone who makes him known to us. Through Jesus Christ we learn that God is our friend, here again not so much by what Jesus Christ said as by what he did. His life, and especially his death, are our witness. Jesus Christ himself is the revelation of God's friendship. So we say not only that we believe in God but that we believe in Jesus Christ.

Teaching. Even this word must not be too exclusively thought of as accepting another person's statements. Teaching is a way of "handing on" something from generation to generation, whether it be a skill, or a mode of behavior, or knowledge in the form of statements. The Catholic Church "hands on" Jesus Christ to us not merely by explicitly telling us about him, but by keeping alive his witness, by teaching us to live and die as he lived and died, to love as he loved. We must remember that the Church is not only the Pope and the bishops and the clergy. *We* are all of us the Church, and *we* teach and witness to the world that God is the friend of men. To believe in the Catholic Church

36

is first and foremost to believe that God's love for man which revealed itself in Christ, still reveals itself in the Church.

Authority. When we think of authority we spontaneously think of the kind of authority that lays down the law and punishes us if we disobey. The Church lays down the law about what we must believe, and can excommunicate us if we refuse to believe. But there is a deeper meaning to authority: as, for example, when we say that Einstein was a world-authority on relativity. This means that Einstein could offer us truth, and if we refuse to listen our punishment is simply to be deprived of that truth. Similarly, the Church is the world-authority on Jesus Christ, and if we refuse to listen to her our punishment is to deprive ourselves of the ability to recognize God as our friend. We lose faith.

Let us therefore remember that faith is not just a matter of dogma. It is the gift of being able to recognize God's overtures and to accept his friendship as revealed to us in Jesus and in the community of our fellow Christians.

What are the chief things which God has revealed?

The chief things which God has revealed are contained in the Apostles' Creed.

Say the Apostles' Creed.

I believe in God, the Father almighty, creator of heaven and earth;

and in Jesus Christ, his only Son, our Lord, who was conceived by the Holy Spirit, born of the virgin Mary, suffered under Pontius Pilate, was crucified, died, and was buried. He descended into hell; the third day he rose again from the dead; he ascended into heaven, and sits at the right hand of God, the Father almighty, from thence he shall come to judge the living and the dead.

I believe in the Holy Spirit, the holy catholic Church, the communion of saints, the forgiveness of sins, the resurrection of the body, and life everlasting. Amen.

How is the Apostles' Creed divided?

The Apostles' Creed is divided into twelve parts or articles.

We said earlier that our faith, hope, and charity towards God are like the belief, trust, and love a wife or husband must have towards his or her partner if life together is to be happy and fruitful. Faith is not simply accepting certain dogmas; it is believing in God, having faith in God as one's friend.

But, of course, someone may ask a married person to say more fully why he has such faith in his partner, and then, with great difficulty, he will try to formulate his *experience* of his partner's love into *statements* about it. I have faith in my partner, he might say, because she has been good to me in this or that way, because there has been this gift or that act of affection. But always such formulation of reasons seems very abstract compared with the experience itself.

So it is with us in the Church. We have faith in God because God *revealed* himself as our friend on Calvary, a friendship *witnessed* to in the life of Jesus, in the life of the apostles, and in the life of Christians in the Church through the ages.

But we in the Church have been asked through the centuries to formulate more fully why we have such faith in God. It has been very difficult, and the result—to be found in the Church creeds and the decrees of ecumenical councils—always seems very abstract compared with the experience of God in Christ which we are trying to describe.

The catechism chooses the shortest and most basic formulation: what we call the Apostles' Creed, not because the Apostles actually wrote it, but because it does formulate *their* experience of God in Christ as they have handed it down in the Church.

Thus, to understand the Creed we should start in the middle: "I believe in Jesus Christ, our Lord." We might note that we never say in the creed, "I believe that such and such a thing happened or that such and such a thing is true." We say, "I believe in *Jesus* who is such and such, or to whom such and such happened." All *facts* mentioned are mentioned as reasons for having faith in a *person*. So it is in our friend Jesus the man that we believe: conceived, born, suffering, dying, and being buried like other men. It is in our friend Jesus, King and Lord, that we believe: rising, ascending to sit with God, and coming to judge us. It is in our friend Jesus, Son of the Father Creator, that we believe: he who sends the Spirit to weld us into the community of the Church, to forgive our sins, raise our bodies, and bring us to everlasting life.

Every article of the Creed describes Jesus, manifests him as our friend, and manifests that in him God befriends us. Dogmas are simply facts manifesting God in this way; thus dogmas can be more or less important. Those facts which are basic to the manifestation of God as our friend are the most important; facts less necessary to such manifestation are less important.

In the course of history both greater and lesser facts get questioned, but because a lesser fact has been defended by the Church does not make it suddenly a greater fact. The articles of the Creed are the great facts; facts like the Assumption or the Immaculate Conception one might indeed call "articles of faith," but they are not articles of the Creed. They are lesser facts: certainly facts, but not of such importance as the ones the catechism considers.

Finally, the Creed is arranged around the three persons of the Trinity, around our three friends. For in Jesus not only the second person of the Trinity befriended us, but also his Father and their Spirit.

Christian life, when lived properly, is a life of having faith in the companionship of these three persons; the Creed is an abstract attempt to formulate the basis and structure of this friendship.

PART ONE

GOD THE FATHER

What is the first article of the Creed?

The first article of the Creed is: "I believe in God, the Father almighty, creator of heaven and earth."

What is God?

God is the supreme spirit, who alone exists of himself, and is infinite in all perfections.

Why is God called almighty?

God is called almighty because he can do all things: "With God all things are possible."

Why is God called creator of heaven and earth?

God is called creator of heaven and earth because he made heaven and earth and all things, out of nothing, by his word.

The Apostles' Creed is the basic Christian act of faith. But a Christian's act of faith is not so much a proclamation of assent to certain dogmas, as an oath of fealty to certain persons: to God the Father, God the Son, and God the Holy Spirit, and a pledge of fidelity to the way they are working in us.

So the first article of the Creed does not say," I believe *that* God the Father almighty created heaven and earth, I assent to this fact." It says, "I believe *in* God, the Father almighty, who is creating heaven and earth, I put my faith in this person, I pledge my fidelity to what he is doing creatively within and around me."

Four words have been used to describe the person in whom I put my faith: he is God, he is Father, he is almighty, and he is creator.

Father. While the catechism later expands on the other three words, it does not comment further on this one. Is this perhaps because the word *Father* names the person to whom I swear faith or fealty, while the other words try to explain what kind of person this Father is? When a Britisher swore fealty to Queen Victoria, the head of his state, he might have been called on to explain further what he meant by "Queen" or "head of state," but he would not have been called on to explain why he called her Victoria. That was just her name. "Father" is the name of the person in whom the Christian puts his faith, to whom he pledges fidelity. *God, almighty,* and *creator* are words used to describe the Father's position in the world and his relation to us.

God. This is the most difficult of the four words. Let us try to explain it. I can ask questions about every single thing I meet in the world. I can even ask why it exists, since I can see that it could have been different. Science-fiction, for example, systematically imagines *different* worlds, and so shows up the arbitrariness of the actual world we live in. Nothing that we meet can make the absolute claim that *it* had to be; something else might have existed in its place. Even the whole world might have been different.

Yet at no time could there ever have been absolute nothingness, for from absolute nothingness existence could never get started at all. Absolute nothingness would make it impossible for the world ever to come to exist. So somebody who says that possibly once there was absolute nothingness, is saying that possibly once our world was impossible! This is obviously a silly statement, because if our world is here, it certainly was never impossible.

This argument leads us to God, because if nothing in our world has to exist, and yet *absolute* nothingness is impossible, then there must be something *outside* our world that has to exist. This is what we call God.

This is what the catechism means when it says that God is the one thing that exists of itself (that is, exists because it must exist), and that all other things exist out of nothing (that is, exist when they did not need to).

Creator. But the catechism goes further, for things that need not exist can only be brought into existence by the one thing that always has to exist: everything else than God must derive from God by God's free act (otherwise they too would be necessary in some way). So we realize that God is a free agent, a person; that the world does not flow out necessarily from God, but is created by him.

Of course, in all this we are only getting at God very indirectly. We are deducing him, so to speak, not meeting him face to face. We are saying that he must be there "back" of the world, and stammering out very imperfect descriptions of him in really quite inadequate words. But this is not yet anywhere near what we mean when we say that we *believe* in him, that we put our faith in him, that we pledge our fidelity to him.

When, as Christians, we say that we believe in God, we do not just mean that we believe some things about him, but that we face up to him, meet him "through" his creation, respond to him as he creates us. This is why the catechism stresses that God created all things "by his word." For when God creates us he is actually speaking to us in some way, he is calling us. Our response to this call must be an acceptance of his word, an acceptance of our creation and a cooperation with it: our response to his creative call is our faith.

Now we can see better what the first article of the Creed is saying. "I believe in the Father," it says. "I pledge my fidelity to his creative activity. I put my faith in the word he speaks to me when as almighty creator-God he brings me into being."

45

Had God any beginning?

God had no beginning: he always was, he is, and he always will be.

Where is God?

God is everywhere.

Does God know and see all things?

God knows and sees all things, even our most secret thoughts.

Has God any body?

God has no body: he is a spirit.

But we must say a little more about the meaning of the word *God*. We said above that, since nothing in our world has to exist and yet *absolute* nothingness is impossible, there must be something *outside* our world that has to exist. This we called God.

Now this concept of God as *outside* the world is today under heavy attack. For example, Bishop John Robinson of Woolwich, in his book *Honest to God,* used arguments from three Protestant theologians (Bultmann, Bonhoeffer, and Tillich) to criticize the idea that God is "out there."

Of course, as Robinson agrees, nobody means by this phrase that God is in outer space; and the Soviet astronaut who announced that he did not find God "up there" was indulging in a cheap sneer. We say that God is *outside* the world not in the sense of being *inside* an outer space (or any other further space we can imagine). He is outside space altogether, not in space at all; and this is because he is creating space.

The same must be said of time. We often talk of God as existing *before* time began and *after* time ends. Since "before" and "after" are time-words, this might suggest that God exists in some "outer time." But God is outside time altogether, he exists apart from time, because he is creating it.

However, there is a subtler meaning to "a God out there," which does not involve a God in outer space or outer time, but which Robinson would still criticize. It is the idea that when God *acts* in the world he acts on it, so to speak, from outside; he intervenes. In Bultmann's words, God is thought of as acting *between* or *over the heads of* ordinary natural events, when he should be thought of as acting *within* them. It is this kind of thinking which leads Tillich to say that God is not another "Being" alongside the world, but is "the infinite and inexhaustible depth and ground of all being."

But is not this image equally odd and liable to abuse? If God is within things is he curled up inside them? Is he to be thought of as part of them? Perhaps Tillich's description "infinite and inexhaustible" is meant to suggest that God is *beyond* all depths of things. But then surely he must also be *beyond* all space and time? And how is he beyond except by being the creator of the depths of things?

The truth is that God is a mystery, and in talking of him we find it very difficult to keep our balance. But we believe that the true Christian tradition—and the catechism is here enshrining it—has kept such a balance. On the one hand, it denies that God is a part of the world by saying that he has *no* body (and therefore *no* place) and had *no* beginning (and therefore *no* existence in time). Yet it sees God present within the world by his creative power, for it says that he is present to all space (everywhere), present to all time (always was and will be), and interior to all things (even our most secret thoughts). One might call this an "all *and* nothing" concept of God, God is *no* thing (and here we find points of agreement with atheists against all crude religions), but he is a "no thing" that is present to *all* things. We might try to put this concept in another way. All our ways of talking about God are images. Now if these images are understood too positively they will always lead us astray, because no worldly image can comprehend God. They are of things, and God is no thing. Thus if "outside the world" is taken positively to mean that God is in some outer space, then it is wrong.

But if we understand the same images in a negative way, then at least they point to God, though never negatively enough. Thus if "outside the world" is taken negatively to mean that God is not *inside* space at all, then at least it helps us to know something of what God is not!

Perhaps we could try to combine both images ("outside" and "inside") and say that God is "at the back of" everything. The world is God seen in a mirror, so to speak; God is a whole universe of which we only see the back in this world.

This would still be an image, and as such it could be misleading; and because it can be misleading, it is even fair, I think, to call it a *myth* about God (which is what most modern authors say). But then we must always remember that such myths are useful negatively even when they are misleading positively; and in fact, apart from the very special way in which God reveals himself in Jesus Christ, they are our only useful ways of talking about God.

In Christ, of course, something new happened which transforms all our myths about God, for in Christ God became *incarnate*. That is to say, the world—or at least that part of the world which was Jesus Christ—now informs us about God in quite a different way. Apart from Christ, the world is something to deduce God from, to suggest images for him, to help us talk about him. But in Christ, the world has become something which we can only call the "body" of God. Just as a man's body is his means of communicating to others who and what he is, and what he is thinking, and what he is feeling, so the world has become not just information *about* God but communication *with* him. But of this matter we shall speak more fully later.

Let us realize that Robinson and Bultmann and Tillich and Bonhoeffer have something really valuable to say to us, and something that is really quite in accord with the whole Christian tradition. For it is true, as Bonhoeffer suggests, that men are always prone to misunderstand the idea that God is "outside" the world. We often take it to mean that God is only out there on the edges of our world. At the limits of understanding or power, when men become puzzled and afraid of the empty abysses opening up around them, there they put God. God is used to cushion men against the infinity of life. But now that man's understanding and power seem to be growing without end, God—as a cushion against life—is dead.

However, the Father of Jesus Christ never intended himself to be a cushion against life, but rather a call to live, a call to man to be himself. God is back of our world pushing us on, and also in front of the world (when it turns in the right direction) pulling us forward. He is not part of the world, but he penetrates it through and through with his creative presence and with his call to us to be men.

Is there only one God?

There is only one God.

Are there three persons in God?

There are three persons in God: God the Father, God the Son, and God the Holy Spirit.

Are these three persons three Gods?

These three persons are not three Gods: the Father, the Son, and the Holy Spirit are all one and the same God.

What is the mystery of the three persons in one God called?

The mystery of the three persons in one God is called the mystery of the Blessed Trinity.

What do you mean by a mystery?

By a mystery I mean a truth which is above reason, but revealed by God.

The mystery of the Trinity is not simply the puzzle of how one can be three and three one. It is rather the revelation that in God, as in our universe, there are giant forces at play, but that in God these giant forces are also personal relationships. First, there is the relationship of Father giving birth to Son; and secondly, there is the relationship of Father and Son together breathing out the Holy Spirit.

To understand this concept let us reflect that there are also two great processes at work in our universe. First, there is the process of evolution by which an original cosmic chaos has given birth to man, the climax of the evolutionary process. We can say that evolution was the world fathering mankind. The second process, in which mankind begins to cooperate with the world that fathered him, we call human history. Where evolution was blind, history is aware of itself; where evolution was dumb, history can express itself in words. Mankind, so to speak, gives the world a vision and a voice. The cooperation of mankind and the world is directed towards a new kind of community that will be the climax of history, namely, the community of a fully civilized universe.

If we were to give a summary account of all this we might say that though there is only one universe, this one universe is built up in two processes. First, the world fathers man, and then man and the world in dialogue produce civilization. The three stages of the universe—the fathering world, man born of the world, and the final civilization—are not three universes, but one and the same universe. The world is the universe in its beginning, man is the universe at the point of achieving self-awareness and expression, and civilization is the universe striving towards a perfect community of love and peace.

Now God himself is such a universe. There is in him a vast Fatherhood, the might of which far transcends the might of created evolutionary forces. For this Fathering is the free and eternal and omnipotent source of all life, while evolution is bound to time and matter. What is born from this vast Fatherhood we call the Son; and in the Son is expressed or put into Word all that is implicit in the Father.

Finally, just as the dialogue of world and man is directed towards the perfect love and peace of a fully civilized universe, so in God the dialogue of Father and Son (now no metaphorical dialogue, but a truly personal one) breathes forth the eternal Spirit of love and peace, the bond of divine community. And this Spirit, too, is God.

The universe has its threefold pattern only because God has it first. And this is what God revealed to us in the mystery of the Trinity. Of course, in all this we have not really "met" the Trinity. We have, in fact, simply given an image taken from our world, a mythical image, so to speak. By itself such an image can be totally misleading. But it is not to be taken by itself. It is only a help to our minds, a sort of suggestion about what it is we meet when, in Jesus Christ, we encounter the Trinity for the first time.

Is there any likeness to the Blessed Trinity in your soul?
> There is this likeness to the Blessed Trinity in my soul: that
> as in one God there are three persons, so in my soul there
> are three powers.

Which are the three powers of your soul?
> The three powers of my soul are my memory, my understand-
> ing, and my will.

Before we talk about meeting the Trinity, let us try to carry
our image further. So far we have discovered a likeness to the
Trinity in the great drama of our universe, for we have seen that
there are two great processes at work in the universe: one, evolution, by which the world has gradually fathered mankind and
so for the first time achieved a self-awareness; and the second,
history, in which man and the world strive together towards the
perfected community of a civilized universe.

In this drama we have discerned a likeness to the drama of
God, in which the Father eternally expresses himself in a Son,
and Father and Son together eternally breathe forth the Spirit
of love and peace, the bond of the divine community.

Now each human life repeats in miniature the whole drama
of the universe into which it is born. For every man is the
product of an immense past made up of his immediate family
background, the culture of the people he belongs to, the long
centuries of mankind's development, and the millenniums of
evolution which preceded it. All this each man carries in himself, not necessarily as explicitly remembered, but as a sort of

unconscious *memory* which we call his tradition and heredity. It is this tradition and heredity which has fathered him.

Moreover, every man must come to terms with this heredity, must take conscious hold of his tradition, must bring that "un-aware memory" to *understanding*. Then only can he begin to take his adult part in the world, lending his *will* to the world task of striving towards the perfect community of a civilized universe, so that in each human life there is a world of tradition fathering him, a self-understanding deriving from this being fathered, and a will to progress resulting from both; and this is the likeness to the Father, Son, and Holy Spirit that the catechism finds in our memory, understanding, and will.

This then is one way in which we are in the image of the Trinity. But this image is an image like a photograph or a statue, not like the image in a mirror. That is to say, it offers a *parallel* in ourselves to what is going on in God, but it is not an actual reflected *presence* of God in us. But with the coming of Jesus Christ, the world and ourselves become an image of the Trinity in this second sense. The Trinity becomes *present* in us and in the world.

Christ has revealed to us that the drama of the universe does more than just imitate the Trinity; it also shares in the very drama of the Trinity itself. The Christian sees in the long process of fathering mankind not merely an imitation of God the Father eternally giving birth to his Son, but sees also that the coming to be of mankind is only the first part of the coming to be in time of God the Son as man.

Again, the process of history is not just a this-worldly striving of man and the world towards a civilized society: a striving which imitates the eternal breathing forth of the Spirit of love and peace by Father and Son. On Calvary the Father and Son breathed that very Spirit into our human history, and it now blows through the world and makes it possible for us to strive towards a community which includes God himself.

Again, it is true that every human life imitates the Trinity, but it is also true that every Christian's life actually shares in the life of the Trinity. In fact, the life of every man who accepts God's actions in history shares in God's life, for such a man is one who accepts these actions as part of his heredity and tradition, incorporates them into his understanding of himself, and allows them to govern his will and its striving.

In this way the act by which the Father gave birth to his Son in time becomes part of every Christian's heredity, and the act by which both breathe forth the Spirit of love and peace becomes the animating principle of every Christian's activity, the wind that blows through him.

This is still not all. For as history progresses we shall enter more and more into the presence of the Trinity. Already now the Spirit breathes in us and relates us closely to the Father and the Son. But we look forward to an even more immediate presence to the Son when he shall come again; and then he shall carry us into face-to-face presence to his Father. All this the Creed will teach us as we go through it.

So when the catechism says that "as in one God there are three persons, so in my soul there are three powers," it is not thinking of a sheerly mathematical parallel. Rather, the catechism is saying that every man's life is a drama of bringing his "memories" or heredity to a state of self-understanding so that he can will his future; that this drama is imitating and sharing in the whole drama of the universe in which the world of the past comes to self-awareness in man and then drives forward to civilization; and, finally, that this drama of the universe in its turn is imitating and sharing in the drama of God: Father bearing Son, and both breathing forth the Spirit of love.

When in the first article of the Creed we swear our fealty to the Father and pledge our fidelity to his creative action within us, we are actually declaring our willingness to respond to a tremendous call—the call to enter into the drama of the Trinity itself. We are called to receive the Spirit from Christ, to strive with the Spirit's help to become more and more a son to the Father, and thus to come face to face with him for ever.

The Creed is our pledge of fidelity, our oath of fealty to God. In the first article we pledged that fealty to God the Father; now in the second we pledge it to his Son. These are not two pledges but one and the same pledge. For we only encounter the Father through the Son, and so can only pledge ourselves to the Father by pledging ourselves to the Son.

THE PERSON OF JESUS CHRIST

What is the second article of the Creed?
The second article of the Creed is: "and in Jesus Christ, his only Son, our Lord."

Who is Jesus Christ?
Jesus Christ is God the Son, made man for us.

Is Jesus Christ truly God?
Jesus Christ is truly God.

Why is Jesus Christ truly God?
Jesus Christ is truly God because he has one and the same nature with God the Father.

Was Jesus Christ always God?
Jesus Christ was always God, born of the Father from all eternity.

Which person of the Blessed Trinity is Jesus Christ?
Jesus Christ is the second person of the Blessed Trinity.

The first article of the Creed was "I believe in God, the Father," and we saw that the principal meaning of this affirmation was: "I put my faith in God the Father and I pledge my fidelity to him." But we may ask, "Where is the Father?", as Philip did at the Last Supper when he said, "Show us the Father." To this we have the answer of Jesus Christ: "He who has seen me has seen the Father; I am in the Father and the Father in me."

In Jesus, the Father has, so to speak, reproduced himself in the form of a man; given birth to a Son of the same nature as himself. In Jesus Christ God has been made man and sent to us, in order that we men might encounter God. "I am the way, the truth, and the life; no one comes to the Father except through me."

Of course, the Father reveals himself to us in *everything* that he has made. This is true. He is the creator of the universe, and therefore the heavens and earth proclaim him and show forth the work of his hands. He is also the creator of mankind, and therefore speaks in man's history as any author speaks in the play he has written. But there is a difference between such revelation of the Father in the world or in history, and the revealing of the Father in his sending of Jesus Christ to us.

The difference is like the difference between listening to a man talking a foreign language and listening to a man whose language we understand. In the first case, the man's behavior will tell us he is a man, not a worm or a whale or a monkey; we see from his behavior that he has human capabilities and a human nature. But because we do not know his language, we do not know the thoughts and desires of his heart.

Similarly, God speaks in creation, but as long as we do not know his language we can learn only something about God's nature. We cannot know the thoughts or desires of God. We can see that the nature of this Creator must far transcend the nature of any of his creatures; he must be all-intelligent and almighty. But not knowing his language, we remain ignorant of what precisely he is trying to say.

The importance of Jesus Christ is that through him God teaches us his language. Jesus Christ is, so to speak, the textbook of God's language. If we learn him, study the textbook, then the language of God in the whole of creation becomes plain. We can turn and see the world with new eyes, and perceive God's thoughts and desires at work in everything he has done.

Jesus Christ, we might say, is the key to God's heart. Jesus' life (and above all his death) has shown us not only what God is abstractly, but who God wants to be in our lives. Jesus has not only displayed God's nature as a life of eternal loving and giving, but he has also shown us that God loves us, devotes himself to our welfare, has made a gift of his entire self to mankind. "In this the love of God was made manifest in us, that God sent his only Son into the world so that we might live through him."

Here we might reflect that although we say God became man in Jesus Christ, we do not say that in Jesus Christ the Father became man, but rather that he sent his Son as man. Why we say this becomes clear, I think, if we hark back to our suggested picture of the Trinity. We compared the process by which the Father gives birth to Son in God with the process of evolution on earth, in which the universe fathers mankind. Now the reason why mankind brings the process of evolution to its achieved climax is because in man the process of evolution becomes conscious of itself for the first time, can reflect upon itself, and through this self-reflection become something different, namely, the process of history. That is why we find in evolution a parallel to the birth of God the Son from God the Father. In the Son the Father produces a reflection of himself, or better, a reflection upon himself. The Father gives birth to someone whose whole life consists in returning upon the Father, in giving living conscious expression to the Father.

We talk often of the Father "speaking" his Son, of the Son as being the Word "spoken by" the Father. But this is not a word such as we speak, which does not *hear* that it is spoken, or cooperate with the speaker. Rather, we must think of the Son on the model of a word which has entered into a sympathetic listener, has become a responsive understanding to the original speaker. The Son is a Word which is listening and responding to its Speaker. Everything that the Speaker has to say is present in this Word; both Speaker and Word are fully God. But in the Father God speaks, and in the Son God listens and responds.

This, then, is why it is the Son who has become man in Jesus Christ; for it is the listening, responding God who has come among us. God speaks and Jesus listens, but listens so perfectly that we know we are in the presence of the divine listening, the eternal listening and responding to God that we call the Son. He has come to sweep us up also into this listening so that we too can hear the Father in the Son. Hence it is that through the Son—God listening among us—we come to know the Father—God speaking to us.

In the Creed, therefore, we affirm our belief not only in the Father, but also in Jesus Christ, his only Son, our Lord. For we could not put our full faith in the Father's love unless we had come to know that love in his Son, and put our faith in that Son. Pledging our fealty to the Father is only possible by pledging fealty to Jesus Christ, in whom the Father is offering himself to us. That is why we must take Jesus Christ, the Father's only Son, as our Lord.

Is Jesus Christ truly man?

Jesus Christ is truly man.

Why is Jesus Christ truly man?

Jesus Christ is truly man because he has the nature of man, having a body and soul like ours.

Was Jesus Christ always man?

Jesus Christ was not always man. He has been man only from the time of his Incarnation.

What is meant by the Incarnation?

By the Incarnation we mean that God the Son took to himself the nature of man: "the Word was made flesh."

We have seen in what sense Jesus is God. We now turn to consider that he was just as truly a man. The apostles, of course, would find this order of doing things rather odd. Jesus Christ as man was their starting point. Only after a great deal of experience of him were they brought to recognize that he was also God.

But for us there is a real reason for approaching Jesus the other way round. Until one sees that Jesus is God one does not see the full meaning of his life, one does not grasp its full sense. So we have started with the truth about Jesus that reveals him most fully and makes clear his role in our human history. The only trouble is that as Christians have more and more understood Jesus to be God, they have found it correspondingly difficult to hold on to Jesus as man. We proclaim that Jesus is man with our lips, but does it really take hold of our hearts?

We must admit that it is easier to proclaim with our lips that

63

"Jesus Christ is truly man" than to acknowledge it in our hearts. For to be truly a man is to be feeble and limited, at the mercy of the world. We cannot help feeling that the Almighty did not really put on feebleness, that the Creator only appeared to put himself at the mercy of the world. We tend to think that in Jesus Christ God *disguised* himself as a man, rather than really become a man.

Why else does it make us uncomfortable to read in the epistle to the Hebrews: "In the days of his flesh Jesus offered up prayer and entreaty, with loud cries and tears, to him who had the power to save him from death, and he was heard for his godly fear. Although he was a Son, he learned to obey through suffering."

The apostles knew the difficulty, but from the other side. They knew Jesus the man, and they were faced with the well-nigh incredible fact that this undoubted man was also God. They had to learn to recognize his being God, not as something alongside his being a man, but as something revealed precisely *in the way he was a man*. They saw that only God could be a man so perfectly.

Being a man is a hard task and a long process; it takes time really to be a man. From childhood, through adolescence, into middle age, one is always learning to be a man. True, from the beginning one is human, in the sense that one is *called* to live a human life and not a cow's life. But to realize that humanity, to respond to that call, is a task which takes a great deal of time.

When we say that God became man, we mean that God chose to take on himself this task, to grow into humanity in this way; at every stage he performed the task perfectly, but he went through the stages like all men do. As Luke says, "Jesus grew in wisdom, in stature, and in favor with God and men."

That last phrase, "in favor with God and men," shows that the task of giving oneself to one's nature, becoming fully human, involves the task of giving oneself to one's fellow men, and also of giving oneself to God, the creator of men. Jesus, in his human life, gave himself to his fellow men and to God in more and more perfect ways, and this reached a climax in the way he died. It was this perfect fulfillment of the task of being a man which revealed that Jesus was God. The centurion at the foot of the cross, "seeing that he thus breathed his last, said, 'Truly this man was the Son of God.'"

Jesus was so perfectly a man that his disciples saw that he was God. He so sacrificed himself to that human love which alone perfects and realizes human life, that men were led to believe they saw not only human love but divine love at work. They were seeing that divine love which shaped the world and man, and which from all eternity has been the divine life.

So the two things are true together: God really became a finite man, while remaining at the same time an infinite God. Indeed, unless we see the two things together we do not grasp the true meaning of either. If we believe that Jesus is God in such a way that we find it difficult to conceive of him being a man, then we have not really grasped the kind of God that is revealed to us in Christ. Our own limited ideas of what God must be are holding us back. Or again, if we believe that Jesus was a man in such a way that we find it difficult to conceive of him being God, then we have not grasped the perfection of man revealed to us in Christ.

We must learn to see the infinity of God precisely in that limitless and generous love with which he chose to be man. However, the fact that God chose *freely* and *generously* to be a feeble man did not make the man he chose to be any *less* feeble.

After all, a great horseman riding a donkey remains a great horseman, and yet by his free choice he has prevented himself from fully showing this fact. But after a time we can discern, even in the way he rides a donkey, that he is an expert rider.

God's infinite power is indeed manifested precisely in the way he conquered the world with a man's weakness; and when we compromise the real humanity of Jesus, we compromise his real divinity also.

To summarize, we could say that Jesus was the greatest of the saints. Two things are at work in all saints: the wind of the Holy Spirit which blows through the world from God, and the bird of human free will which consents to that wind and rides on it triumphantly. In Christ too these two things were at work: his obedience as a man responded to the grace of his Father's Spirit, and so became the window through which the whole infinite power of that Spirit was released to blow through the world.

Let us, then, learn to know and love Jesus as a man, and not only as God. Let us learn to know and love him as the greatest man there has been in the world: one who in the middle of trial and weakness reached the summits of human love and human achievement.

How many natures are there in Jesus Christ?

There are two natures in Jesus Christ, the nature of God and the nature of man.

Is there only one person in Jesus Christ?

There is only one person in Jesus Christ, which is the person of God the Son.

Faith is not simply a matter of believing dogmas, but of putting faith in God as a friend; and the Apostles' Creed is therefore not so much a recounting of facts as a putting into words of our personal relationship to the Father, the Son, and the Holy Spirit.

But, of course, in putting into words our relationship to a person it is often necessary to recount facts about him, especially facts that are misrepresented or misunderstood. Thus from time to time the Church formulates dogmatic pronouncements, so phrased as to remove whatever doubts are uppermost in men's minds at the time.

Because she has the promised assistance of the Holy Spirit, these pronouncements are valid for all time; but because they are reactions to particular historical situations, they can only properly be understood in the light of those situations.

In the last few catechism questions we have been talking of our encounter with Jesus—the Son who shows us the Father, the man whom God is. The Church has dogmatically expressed this truth by saying that the one person of Jesus Christ is of two distinct natures: God and man. The catechism goes on to consider this formulation.

Does it mean that Jesus is something like Dr. Jekyll and Mr. Hyde—somebody with a split personality, as we should say nowadays, who at one moment behaves in one way and at another in an entirely different way? But we have seen that Jesus does not alternate between being God and being man; it is just precisely by being man perfectly that Jesus shows that he is God.

Nor is Jesus like a mule, which combines at one and the same time the two natures of horse and donkey. The word *nature* derives from the Latin verb "to be born." Nature is what you are given at birth, the sort of thing you are born to be. Dr. Jekyll and the mule were only born once, so that their apparent double natures are really only the one nature they were born with.

In order to make it clear that Jesus did not have only one nature (as the Monophysite heretics had said), the Church stresses the fundamental fact that Jesus was born twice. In eternity he is the Son of his Father, born into a ·divine nature; and at a moment of time he was born from the virgin Mary, born into a human nature.

Yet it was the same person born both times. Against the Nestorians, who thought of Christ as two persons, the Church had to remind us that though Christ was *born* twice, he did not *come into existence* twice. With us birth is not only the moment of getting our nature, but also of coming into existence. But Jesus has existed from all eternity (which is why we call his person divine), and yet he has been born twice, once eternally into a divine nature, and a second time historically into a human nature.

So this is the core of what the Church is teaching: that Jesus was born twice, yet did not come into existence twice. To deny this teaching would be to fall into heresy. Yet it is not heresy to discuss what might be called the inevitable "imperfections" of the way we formulate this truth. This is a very important point to understand. We are as Christians bound to believe the truth which we are trying to formulate in human language; we are equally bound to disbelieve that human language can ever *perfectly* formulate this truth. Just as we said on page 20 above that we know our words for God are true without quite knowing what they mean, and just as we said on page 46 that we must confess God to be "outside" the world while at the same time recognizing the word "outside" to be positively misleading in certain respects, so now we say that Jesus Christ was born twice, though we must beware of pressing the word *twice* too far.

Just as God is "outside" this world, not as being "inside" some other world alongside ours, but simply as not-being-contained by our world, so also the eternal birth of Jesus is not "another" birth from his human birth in the sense that it happens in some other time alongside ours, but simply in the sense that it is not contained by our time at all. On the other hand, just as the reason why God is not contained in our world is because he is its creator and therefore more deeply present within the world than the world itself is, so also the reason why the eternal birth of Jesus is not contained in any moment of our time is because he is the creator of time and so deeply present to it that it cannot capture him in its own limitations.

The human birth of Jesus is, in fact, an incarnation, a "making flesh" of his eternal birth. But the "making flesh" differs from what is made flesh, and so we say that there are two births. Yet one is the realization in history of the other, and so the two births are not entirely divorced from one another.

An example might make this clearer. Helen Keller was born totally deaf and blind and therefore unable to speak. Through the patience of her parents and her nurse she was brought, one blissful day, to a sudden realization of what a word was; the world of language dawned on her as she held her hands under running water from a tap, and the word *water* was spelled out on her palm. It was a new birth into a new world, a second birth, and yet a birth which only realized for the first time the potentialities of her first birth.

In the case of Helen Keller we think of the second birth as only metaphorically a birth, precisely because it was already totally implicit in her first and real birth. But in the case of our own baptisms we have an example of a second birth which is not just metaphorical but real. We wake into a new world; and it really is a new world breaking out beyond all the limitations of our first birth. We see a new light and hear a new language; and yet it is the same person who was born from his mother's womb who is now born again from the baptismal font.

Now these two births of ours are exactly the two births of Jesus. In baptism we were born from above, born sons of God, as he was born from above; and at our human birth we were born from below, born sons of earth, as he too was born from below. The difference lies in the order of the births. Because our divine birth supervenes on our human birth, we are fundamentally human persons born again into a divine world; because his human birth supervened upon his divine birth, he is fundamentally a divine person born again into a human world. Yet in him, just as in us, the two births are related and united to one another so that one is the making flesh of the other.

Besides the inevitable "imperfection" of any dogmatic formulation—represented here by the ambiguities of the word *twice*—we also find in any dogma the mark of the historical period in which it was first formulated. In what we have been saying, for example, the word *person* has a significance which is not entirely the same as that which the word most commonly has today. We have been using it to mean that despite Jesus' two births, he has only one existence. "Person"—he who exists—is very clearly distinguished from "nature"—what he is born to. But today we often use the word *person* to signify the peculiar characteristics of human "nature." When, for example, we say of someone that he has become quite a different person, we are referring to that growth in self-possession and self-command which is, or should be, characteristic of a human life. In this sense of "person" there can be no doubt that Jesus also was a human person; he too grew during his life towards a fuller and fuller realization of the potentialities that had been humanly born in him. But it was one and the same "person" (in the older sense) that was eternally the Son of the Father and that in his historical life had to grow up as a human "person" (in the newer sense).

Here then is a living example of the strength and weakness of dogmatic formulations. They enshrine truths which we deny on pain of heresy; but they enshrine them in such a way that their terms still have to be discussed century after century, and in such a way that they can never be called "perfect" formulations of the truth they enshrine.

But now we must return from our digression. What the Church is aiming at in this dogmatic formulation is, in the last analysis, an expression of her personal faith in Jesus. To achieve this goal she recounts what may seem an abstract fact about Jesus. What does this fact have to say about our personal relationship with him?

Here we can only provide a very poor analogy. Sometimes in a place all our experience of the characteristics of that place coalesce into a feeling of its particular uniqueness, a sort

71

of feeling of the presence of the place. Fujiyama or the Grand Canyon will give this sort of feeling. If the place is man-made (like Stonehenge in England, or St. Peter's) and especially by someone whom one loves or reveres (one's father's study, let us say, or one's son's bedroom), then over and beyond this feeling of the presence of the *place,* and yet incarnated in it, one feels a direct encounter with the *person* or persons who made it.

Can we suggest that meeting Christ (either in the flesh or in the Church) is something like this? To meet an ordinary man is to feel the presence, in his many different ways of behaving, of one human person. But to meet Christ is to encounter something over and beyond what a human person would be, and yet something encountered directly as incarnate in a human nature.

We meet the person of Christ in his human nature, just as we would meet any other man, but in meeting him we are aware, in faith, that his person goes deeper than any other person we can meet, infinitely and eternally and divinely deeper. We are aware of a creative, divine power coming out of him to remake us in his Father's image; and because of this awareness we are prepared to offer him our total fidelity.

THE WORK OF JESUS

Why was God the Son made man?
  God the Son was made man to redeem us from sin and hell,
  and to teach us the way to heaven.
What does the holy name Jesus mean?
  The holy name Jesus means Saviour.
What does the name Christ mean?
  The name Christ means Anointed.

We have been talking about the person of Jesus, and how he,
a man, is also the Son of God: truly man and truly God, one
person in two natures. Now the catechism asks: but why?
For what reason did God the Son become man?

Already we have broached this question and given a first
answer: because God wanted to reveal himself to man. God
wanted man to know and enjoy not only the universe God had
made, but also the "universe" God himself is. So he put one
universe inside the other, so to speak; he put God in the world
to be met, known, and enjoyed by men.

In our earlier picture of the Trinity, we likened the coming of
the Son of God into the world to the first coming of man into
the universe. When, at the end of the great process of evolution,
man first appeared on earth, the whole universe was suddenly
transformed from within. For the first time it became a place
which could see, love, and enjoy itself from inside. Up till then

there had been no such power of seeing and enjoying in the universe; but now, at its center, there was the spirit of man. And through that spirit, so to speak, the universe could begin to comprehend and appreciate itself.

In man, one could say, the universe began to turn back on itself, to look after itself responsibly for the first time. The first task of man is to care for his own development, and then to care for the development of the universe he lives in, all in the service of God who created both universe and man. This is what the Scripture is teaching us when, at the very beginning of the book of Genesis, it tells us that man was put into the garden of this world to till it and to keep it.

One might indeed say that mankind is a prophet to the universe, that is to say, a light to the material world, a source of revelation in it, which enables it to grasp itself and to make sense of itself. Then again he is a priest to the universe, that is to say, someone who can represent the material world before God and offer thanks for it to its creator. Finally, he is a king to the universe, that is to say, he can organize and rule the universe he lives in for its greater and greater welfare.

Of course, we need only look around to see how far short of these duties man has fallen. The power he was given to serve the universe, he squanders often on private and selfish ends. So the universe has not been fulfilled as it should have been; as St. Paul says, it groans in frustration because of the selfishness of man.

But now God does a new thing. He sends his Son into the world as a man, and when this new man appears on earth, the whole universe is again suddenly transformed from within. For the first time it becomes a place which can see love and enjoy itself from inside as God sees, loves, and enjoys it—even more, as God sees, loves, and enjoys himself.

Jesus, it can be said, is the new Adam, the new man: in him all those neglected tasks of the first Adam are to be fulfilled. But Jesus is also the Son of God. He is not only the point at which the universe of this world can turn back on itself and begin for the first time to look after itself responsibly. He is also the point at which the "universe" of God himself turns back on himself, and he therefore gives to the world into which he has come the power to respond fully to God himself for the first time. He introduces our world into the drama of the Trinity itself, and allows it to take part with him in the eternal self-knowledge and life of love existing in God.

Just as man came into the world not only to care for his own development but also to care for that of the whole universe, so also Jesus is in the world not only so that he might live his life of return and response to his Father, but also that all men and the universe itself might be enabled to share in that response and return. It was the work given to Jesus by his Father to lead the world back to the Father for ever.

Thus Jesus is also prophet, priest, and king, but a much greater prophet, priest, and king than the first man. For he is the light of God, the love of God, the creative power of God abroad in the world. In this new man, therefore, the universe receives not merely the power to care for itself but to recreate itself, to bring itself into the very world of God. The very springs of creation, the very Creator, has come into the universe and into man to give it and him a new center. That is what the catechism means when it says that God became man to teach us the way to heaven: to teach us how to return to the Father, to enter into the "universe" of God while still here in the universe we live in and serve.

By uniting ourselves to Christ, in whom the power of return to the Father has been given us, and who made of his human life among us the instrument of that return to God, we can unite our human work to his. His spirit will then live also in our work; and we can breathe forth into the world the very happiness of God. By so doing we rescue both ourselves and the universe from the frustration under which it groans; we are "redeemed from sin and hell."

Of course, just as the universe cannot love and enjoy itself except in and through man, so also it cannot recreate itself except in and through the man Jesus. But ever since man evolved, the world of matter has been responding to the intelligence within it; and since the Incarnation, all those who unite themselves to Christ are able to respond to his life of love within the world, and to the Holy Spirit of recreation which dwells in that life.

Ever since the Incarnation, and especially since the Resurrection when Jesus fully manifested himself as the way of return to the Father, man has been able to find salvation in Jesus (whose name means "God saves") and to confess him as prophet, priest, and king (which is what his title "the Anointed one, the Christ" really means).

THE BODY OF JESUS

What is the third article of the Creed?

The third article of the Creed is, "who was conceived by the Holy Spirit, born of the virgin Mary."

What does the third article mean?

The third article means that God the Son took a body and soul like ours in the womb of the blessed virgin Mary, by the power of the Holy Spirit.

Had Jesus Christ any father on earth?

Jesus Christ had no father on earth; St. Joseph was only his guardian or foster-father.

Where was our Saviour born?

Our Saviour was born in a stable at Bethlehem.

On what day was our Saviour born?

Our Saviour was born on Christmas Day.

When one divides the creed into twelve articles as the catechism does, then this is indeed the third article. But it would be historically more correct to divide the creed into only *three* articles: I believe in God the Father; I believe in his Son, Jesus Christ; I believe in the Holy Spirit. On such a division we have not yet come to the third article—the article on the Holy Spirit—and what the catechism calls articles three to seven must be treated as appendages to the second article. In other words, they tell us more about Jesus Christ, to whom we have pledged our fealty in article two.

But now we have a problem. Why include our Lord's conception and birth in the Creed at all? What does it tell us about Christ that can be compared in importance with his death and resurrection and ascension and second coming as judge? These latter events were part of the apostolic preaching from the beginning, as we can read in Acts; but why pick out of all the other events of Christ's life this one of his birth, never mentioned in the apostles' preaching at all?

Indeed, only two of the Gospels give an account of Christ's birth, and even in them it is rather loosely attached to the rest of the story. Moreover, Matthew's account differs greatly from Luke's. In fact, many Scripture scholars believe that the two accounts are not eyewitness accounts at all, but more like "parables" about our Lord's birth not meant to be accurate in all their historical details.

Perhaps we will understand this explanation better if we think of the Gospel writers as doing something like the catechism-author does when he tells us that Jesus was born in a stable on Christmas Day. Here he is embroidering a Gospel account which says simply that Jesus was born in a manger, there being no room at the inn. Nothing is said about his birth being in winter: this is an old tradition connecting the birth with the winter solstice, that pagan feast celebrating the return of the sun from the southern hemisphere to the northern one.

Further, the stable-idea derives from meditation on two Old Testament passages, one of which is mistranslated, and neither of which have anything immediately to do with the birth of Christ (Isaiah 1, 3 and Habakkuk 3, 2). But although the details are not historically accurate, they are ways of expressing the undoubted truth that Christ is the sun of the world, born into a world which had no room for him.

To some Scripture scholars it has seemed that many of the Gospel details about Christ's birth are themselves of this sort: teaching us deep truths about Christ which were derived not from eyewitnesses but by meditating on Old Testament texts. And if the catechism can do it (and we, every time we build a crib), why should not the Gospel?

Thus we come back to the question: Why is this event included in the Creed in preference to many better authenticated historical events in Christ's life? Surely the answer is that it is not included precisely as an event, but because of the truth it proclaims about who Christ was.

In the catechism all the questions about the person of Christ who was both God and man occur under the second article, and we have already dealt with them. But in fact the second article of the Creed, as we saw, was not so much a proclamation of dogma as an oath of fealty by which we put our faith in Jesus Christ, the Father's Son, accepting him as our Lord. It is here, in the third article, that the Creed proclaims the dogma of Christ, both God and man; and it does so by saying that he is both Spirit and flesh, conceived of God and born of a woman.

We might note how the Creed, just like the Gospels, stresses the *flesh* when it teaches us of the real humanity of Christ. This does not mean that Christ was without a human soul, but like all men he lived and acted in a body; it was in and through his bodily life that he saved us. Throughout the next articles—from the passion and resurrection of Christ right through to Christ's life in the Church and the general resurrection—we shall continually notice how important that bodily aspect of Christ is in the whole plan of our salvation.

Where is Jesus Christ?

As God, Jesus Christ is everywhere. As God made man, he is in heaven and in the blessed sacrament of the altar.

If Jesus came to show us the Father, if we only encounter the Father through his Son, then it is reasonable to ask: And where do I find this Son? Where is Jesus Christ? He is no longer walking Palestine to be met, touched, seen, and believed in. If I wish to put my faith in him, where do I find him?

At first sight, the catechism answer seems to say: in three places—in one place as God and in two others as man. But how can someone be in three different places? Are we supposed to think of Jesus as something like a businessman with three addresses: his earthly office for interviews, his heavenly home for ordinary living, his mountain retreat for divine solitude?

A more careful look at the catechism answer gives a different picture. For all three places turn out to be the same place. To the question "Where?" the first answer is, "Jesus cannot be limited to any 'where' because he is God"—he is eternally everywhere. But then the catechism goes on: "True, he is also a man, but a man who has returned to God his Father to share with him his everlasting presence to all things and all places"—he is in heaven.

Finally, it adds, "That does not mean that he is 'out of this world'; heaven is as present to the world as God is, but in a hidden way. Thus, thirdly, we can say that Jesus' universal presence manifests itself to us in the world, at certain times and places and in special ways which we call the sacraments."

For, of course, the Eucharistic presence itself is nothing else than the everlasting and all-pervading presence of the Lord, manifested to us in a special way at this time and place. This time and place *manifest* Jesus to us, they do not confine him. In the Eucharist the whiteness and roundness and the confines of the host make present to us here-and-now that Jesus who is not white nor round nor confined to this here-and-now. Indeed, the Eucharistic presence of Jesus in this world is a presence which of its very nature urges us to look beyond it to where Jesus is in heaven. For in the first place it is a hidden presence, a presence under sign, and not an open face-to-face presence. And secondly, the signs themselves are in one sense signs of an absence, for these signs refer to the opening of the Jewish paschal meal—the breaking of bread—and to the close of the same meal—the final cup of blessing—and by so doing they draw our attention to the absence of the main course of the paschal meal, namely, the paschal lamb. This is because the slaying and eating of the paschal lamb—our new paschal lamb, Jesus Christ—belong historically to another time and place than any Mass that we offer, and are present in the Mass not historically but sacramentally. Thus the slaying of the lamb was done on Calvary, 2000 years ago; and the Mass does not *repeat* that slaying, it *makes us present again* to the original slaying. Our eating of the paschal lamb will be completed only in heaven; the Mass does not *repeat* that heavenly eating over and over again, rather it *makes us present* through sign of our actual communion with the risen Christ now to that final eating which is to be ours for ever in heaven.

So Jesus Christ is not in three places. As God he is present in every place in the sense of making himself present in and through that place; but he is in no place in the sense of being confined to it. Because of our bodily nature we can encounter people only if they are somewhere, in some place, to be seen and touched. So God, one might say, "placed" himself for us by becoming a man with a body which was seeable and touchable. To Jesus' contemporaries the place of his body was just like that of any other man's body, limited and confined. In that body and its place God was specially present. At the moment of Calvary and the resurrection especially the place of Jesus' body was the place of God, for at that moment, in that place, God fully revealed himself in the infinity of his love for men. At that moment, in that place, he let himself be seen as the Son, engaged in a return and a response to his Father. The paschal body of Jesus, as we might call it, is the place to which we must always return if we are to see God the Son fully within our world.

This is in fact what the sacramental presence in the Eucharist and the other sacraments allows us to do. It allows us to go back, so to speak, to the paschal body of Jesus. It makes him present again in sign as he was on Calvary and at the moment of his resurrection; it makes him present again in his human body as it was at the moment that it returned to the Father.

Jesus, then, is everywhere. He now encounters us in every manifestation of his Spirit within this world, be it in his saints, or in his sacraments, or in the word of Scripture, or in the teaching of the Church. But, because these ways of presence are themselves countless, they must all be related back to the one historical there-and-then presence of Jesus as he rose again from the dead if they are to be grasped by us as a unified presence.

Thus in his saints we are meeting Christ *re*-presenting his death and resurrection to us through their actions; and in the sacraments we meet him *re*-presenting this same mystery to us under ritual forms. At each moment the universal presence of God revealed to us in the presence of Jesus is available to us, but only insofar as each moment is tied to the great moment when God's full presence was first mediated to us in a worldly event, to the moment of Calvary and the first Easter. This was the moment when earth and heaven were linked.

In the second article of the Creed we swear fealty to the Father, by recognizing Jesus Christ, his Son, as our Lord. That is to say, we pledge ourselves to find Calvary and Easter in every moment of our life; we pledge ourselves to encounter Jesus in his moment of dying and handing on the Spirit in everything that we do and in everything that is done to us.

The Creed now turns to study more closely the flesh of Jesus, the body of Jesus, and especially the body of Jesus at the moment of Calvary and Easter, for it is to this moment we must turn if we are to find the Son returning to his Father, and join him in his return.

What is the fourth article of the Creed?

The fourth article of the Creed is, "suffered under Pontius Pilate, was crucified, died, and was buried."

What were the chief sufferings of Christ?

The chief sufferings of Christ were: first, his agony and his sweat of blood in the garden; second, his being scourged at the pillar and crowned with thorns; and third, his carrying his cross, his crucifixion, and his death between two thieves.

What are the chief sufferings of our Lord called?

The chief sufferings of our Lord are called "the passion of Jesus Christ."

We have preferred to divide the Creed not into twelve articles but into three: "I believe in God the Father"—the catechism's first article; "I believe in Jesus Christ, his only Son"—the catechism's articles two to seven inclusive; and "I believe in the Holy Spirit"—the catechism's articles eight to twelve. So that now, in starting the catechism's article four, we are really in the middle of explaining the second article of our division: our proclamation of fealty to Jesus Christ, our Lord.

We have also seen that the Creed concentrates on "the body of Christ" as the really concrete place of encounter with God. Thus already when teaching that Christ was both God and man, the Creed referred to the being God as being conceived by the Spirit, and to the being man as being born of a woman's flesh. God came down to encounter us, to come into contact with us, and men encounter each other and contact each other through their bodies. So, already for this reason, the body of Jesus is of the highest importance to us. "The Word became flesh," writes St. John. And again: "Something which has existed since the beginning, that we have heard, that we have seen with our own eyes, that we have watched and *touched with our hands*: the Word, who is life—that is our subject."

But in a very special way it is Christ's body at the moment of his departure to the Father—his body on the cross and rising from the tomb—which is our place of encounter with him. For at that moment he revealed to us most fully in his body, at one and the same time, his unity with men and his unity with God his Father. The unity with men was shown in the fact that he could suffer and die—something characteristic of men, and something possible to him because he also had a body. The unity with God was shown in the infinity of love with which this death was embraced—God's love for man, and the Son's love for his Father became visible, so to speak, at that moment. "This has taught us love—that he gave up his life for us."

For the moment let us just think of his sufferings as the mark of his unity with us. "As it was his purpose to bring a great many of his sons into glory," says the epistle to the Hebrews, "it was appropriate that God . . . should make perfect through suffering the leader who would take them to their salvation. . . . Since all the children share the same blood and flesh, he too shared equally in it, so that by his death he could take away all the power of the devil, who had power over death, and set free all those who had been held in slavery all their lives by the fear of death."

All the questions that tend to come into our heads—Was it necessary that Christ should suffer? necessary that he should die? necessary that he should die in just this way?—all these questions must be held back for the time being, and that because the word *necessary* is not really appropriate. People in love do many things that are not necessary, but which bind them as closely as is possible to those they are in love with. Further, we must realize that God became man not, first of all, to fulfill any necessities, but because he was in love with us. He became man, and that means he became a sufferer, he became one who dies, he became one who is persecuted by the world if he tries to remain loyal to the truth.

Thus the Creed finds it of the greatest importance to talk of Christ suffering, of his bodily helplessness. The supreme Spirit took to himself a body, the Creator put himself at the mercy of the world, the totally active God became subject to passiveness and suffering, went through a passion—and this because he had become really one of us in our suffering and bodily helplessness.

It was not that his sufferings were only physical. The body is a gateway through which all kinds of other sufferings can come to us. In the agony in the garden Christ said, "My soul is sorrowful to the point of death." He was deep in the distress we all feel when what *must* be done is not what we would *like* to do. He prayed that the decision might not be asked of him, he wrestled and sweated blood, and came through: "Not my will but yours be done." This was not just physical suffering, but a mental suffering that his body laid him open to.

Again, the scourging and crowning were more than the physical pain of lash and thorns. He was being humiliated by nakedness, stripped of all human dignity, and all he held sacred was being mocked with a make-believe crown and royal robe: "Hail, king of the Jews!"

Finally, the crucifixion "between two thieves" was not just a painful death but also a shameful one reserved for the worst criminals. He died unjustly condemned as a traitor to his country.

It was God who thus suffered, showing himself to be really one of us experiencing with us the common lot of mankind.

Why did our Saviour suffer?

Our Saviour suffered in order to atone for our sins, and to purchase for us eternal life.

Why is Jesus Christ called our redeemer?

Jesus Christ is called our redeemer because his precious blood is the price by which we were ransomed.

We said previously that in order really to become a man like us, God took to himself a suffering body; he suffered so that he could be our brother in everything. But this is only part of the story. By sharing our suffering he has transformed it and will eventually do away with it.

The suffering we are chiefly talking about here is the suffering caused by sin, what has been called "man's inhumanity to man." For sin is inhumanity.

It is the tragedy of humans that they are all also inhumans; made for communication and cooperation and brotherly love, they are unable to stifle in themselves a divisive and destructive spirit which continually denies love and disintegrates humanity.

Every man suffers from this disintegration, suffers sin; and yet every man is also an instrument of disintegration, an instrument of sin. Men seem to be carried along by sin, like tree-trunks in a flood, destroyed themselves and yet themselves wreaking destruction on all they meet.

God became man in order that he also could suffer this inhumanity; he gave himself up to this flood of sin so utterly that St. Paul can describe him as coming "in the likeness of sin-ful flesh," "cursed for our sake," "made into sin." That is to say, he allowed himself to be inundated by the force of sin, to be ravished by human inhumanity. But, as St. Paul also says, without sinning, without himself becoming an instrument of sin.

When men are whirled away by sin they become inhuman, themselves instruments of sin. They cannot stand up against sin's overwhelming force. But Christ came to suffer inhumanity and yet remain human, to absorb that flow of sin *into* himself but not allow it ever to flow *out* from himself. Sin, man's inhumanity, flooded with all its force against him so that in the end it took away his human life; but he received it always with love, always with forgiveness, so that it never took away his humanity. We might say that though he died, he never let death kill him; he *loved* to the end, as St. John says; he was even most truly alive at the moment he was dying.

The suffering body of Jesus was the dwelling place of an infinite love, an undying love; he was indeed Love made flesh. His very death was a triumph of love and therefore a defeat for sin, the first indication to the world that there is a kind of life that even death cannot kill, an undying life, an eternal life. At the moment of his dying to this world, Christ completely realized that eternal life, which is but another name for God's life.

Christ has offered this kind of life to us, too. We shall still die, have to suffer sin, but (if we let him) he will realize in our death that eternal life which is God's. We shall die to this world but live forever in God.

For we will have suffered all the forces of disintegration can do to us, and still have remained "whole." That is why Christ is said to have atoned for sin. The word *atone* comes from the two words *at one*. Sin tries to break us up, to "put us at sixes and sevens"; but through Christ, sin is defeated, we can remain whole, we can remain "at one" with God and our fellow men.

We can use other images. We were "slaves" to disintegration, but now we have been "made free," we have been "ransomed." Sometimes it seems to us that talk about Christ "purchasing, or redeeming (that is, buying back), mankind on the cross" transforms Calvary into a kind of commercial transaction. It sounds as though God, man, and the devil were involved in some business deal, and a rather unsavory one at that. But these words are only metaphors taken from the usual process of freeing slaves. When Christ is described as purchasing life for us with his blood, that means neither more nor less than that he freed us from slavery to sin through his own sufferings.

On what day did our Saviour die?

Our Saviour died on Good Friday.

Where did our Saviour die?

Our Saviour died on Mount Calvary.

Why do we make the sign of the cross?

We make the sign of the cross, first to put us in mind of the Blessed Trinity; and second, to remind us that God the Son died for us on the cross.

In making the sign of the cross, how are we reminded of the Blessed Trinity?

In making the sign of the cross we are reminded of the Blessed Trinity by the words "In the name of the Father and of the Son and of the Holy Spirit."

In making the sign of the cross, how are we reminded that Christ died for us on the cross?

In making the sign of the cross we are reminded that Christ died for us on the cross, by the very form of the cross which we make upon ourselves.

We have said that Christ suffered death in order that we might enjoy eternal life. But what is meant by "eternal life"?

The first meaning that springs to our mind is, of course, "living forever." We all must die, as Christ himself died, but afterwards there is offered to us a life that will never end, a life with God forever in heaven.

But this is only the beginning of the meaning of eternal life. For besides meaning an everlasting life after death, eternal life also means a life that "will never see death," as Jesus said. Here we must understand death to mean not physical death, but that second death that the book of the Apocalypse refers to, the death of being sent to hell, the total death reserved for the wicked.

In the first meaning of the words, we cannot enter into eternal life until after our physical death; but in the second meaning of the words, we can enter into eternal life now. We can receive the gift of being freed from the slavery of sin and the threat of hell even in this life.

This is what was meant when we said that Christ died in such a way that death did not *kill* him; his body was killed on the cross by man's inhumanity, but because he received this inhumanity with love and forgiveness it could never kill *his* humanity, he never succumbed to sin. Thus St. Paul could talk of baptism (in which we clothe ourselves, so to speak, with the spirit of the dying Christ) as giving us already eternal life. "When Christ died, he died once for all to sin: . . . In that way, you too must consider yourselves to be dead to sin and alive for God in Christ Jesus." Thus St. John could talk of eternal life as being not so much in opposition to physical death, but in opposition to being lost, being condemned to hell. "God loved the world so much that he gave his only Son so that everyone who believes in him may not be lost, but may have eternal life."

Yet even all this is not the final meaning of eternal life. When St. John says, "The Word, who is life—this is our subject," he is using "life" as a name for God himself. He continues, "That life was made visible, we saw it and are giving testimony, telling you of the eternal life which was the Father and has been made visible to us." Eternal life is the life lived by Father, Son, and Spirit for all eternity, just as life in time is the life lived by mortal men.

How did this life become visible? It became visible as the love shown by Christ on Calvary; here men saw what sort of person the second person of the Blessed Trinity was, and what sort of life he lived. "God is love; this love was revealed to us . . . when he sent his Son to be the sacrifice that takes our sins away." To live like God is to live wholly a life of love; Christ was love made flesh.

We can put this truth another way. God is eternal life. In the Father this life takes the form of an eternal fathering of a Son, an eternal outpouring of love which gives birth to that second person of the Trinity. In that Son the same life takes the form of an eternal turning towards the Father, an eternal return in love to the person who is giving him birth. Now in Christ both these forms of eternal life are made visible to us in the flesh. During his life the stress is laid on Christ's coming out from the Father, "he who sent me," as Christ calls him. In Christ we see the Father at work fathering his eternal Son in human form. At the moment of his death the stress begins to be laid on Christ's return to the Father: "I am going to him who sent me." It is at this moment especially that we begin to see the fullness of the Son in Christ, see him as the one who is eternally returning in love to his Father. John introduces the last moments of Jesus' life thus: "It was before the feast of the passover and Jesus knew that the hour had come for him to pass from this world to the Father. He had always loved those who were his in the world, but now he loved them to perfection. . . . Jesus knew that the Father had put everything into his hands, and that he had come from God and was returning to God. . . ." Then follows the discourse after the Last Supper in which Jesus explains over and over again to his disciples that it is in his return to the Father that the fullness of his eternal love and eternal life will be made visible on this earth.

So it is that we can say that in the moment of Calvary Christ was the eternal love of Son for Father made flesh. This is the gift given to us on Calvary, to share in that love for the Father and to be prepared for our return to the Father. Christ has given us the power to live like God, to be also love made flesh. He has given us the eternal life of the Trinity, so that "we can be as he is in this world." St. John says, "You will live in the Son and in the Father; what is promised to you by his own promise is eternal life."

In the sign of the cross—as the catechism points out—we have a marvelous token of this promise. First and foremost the cross reminds us of that eternal life which is the Blessed Trinity; and this has been manifested to us in the act of love which was Christ's death on Calvary.

In our baptism that power of love was also given to us, so that we too might manifest it in our death; we too are called to die in such a way that death does not kill us, that the eternal life given to us in baptism goes on living forever, that we return to our Father.

What is the fifth article of the Creed?

The fifth article of the Creed is, "he descended into hell, the third day he rose again from the dead."

What is meant by the words "he descended into hell"?

The words "he descended into hell" mean that as soon as Christ was dead his blessed soul went down into that part of hell called limbo.

What is meant by limbo?

By limbo is meant a place of rest where the souls of the just who died before Christ were detained.

Why were the souls of the just detained in limbo?

The souls of the just were detained in limbo because they could not go up to the kingdom of heaven till Christ had opened it for them.

We need to know some history in order to interpret this article. We cannot see what it means just by looking at it. And its history is quite complicated.

First of all, the phrase "descended into hell" is an old Hebrew idiom, and to them it simply meant "he died." But said of Christ, it recalls many New Testament remarks about Christ's triumph over death, and especially the remark of St. Peter that Christ went, after his death, to preach to "the spirits in prison," to preach to the dead. The phrase was incorporated in the Creed for the first time about the fourth century, and it is a bit of a puzzle why the Church suddenly felt the need of it just then. Finally, the explanation given in the catechism—which refers to "limbo"—makes use of a concept which is even later historically, a concept which came into prominence only in the Middle Ages.

So the history of this article is rather complicated; and we can perhaps unravel it best by going right back into the Old Testament.

"Hell" in the Old Testament is not so much a place or form of life *after* death, as a vivid portrayal of the horrors of death itself. "To descend to hell" was a common Hebrew way of saying "to die" (or even sometimes "to be fatally ill"); it was to go out of life, to lose all the activity and joys of living, to have no future any more.

For, in the Old Testament, man could not look forward to anything after death: nothing was known about what would happen then. There was no idea of either heaven or hell in our sense of the terms. What men hoped for in the Old Testament was as full a life as possible *before* death, not a new life after it. Thus we read there that "all men must descend to hell," all men must die, but some descend peacefully, in a ripe old age, while some die bloodily and untimely, cut off in their prime.

Only with the coming of Christ does somebody break through the dead-end of death. Christ came to that dead-end as every man does, but at the moment of its greatest horror and desolation God brought him through to a new life. He was raised from the dead. And this action of God's created heaven, created a life after death.

We get into great confusion when we try to distinguish heaven and hell and purgatory and limbo as so many different places that have existed from the beginning of creation. Insofar as heaven is God it has, of course, existed from all eternity; but as a human place—the presence of man before God—it has existed only since the resurrection of Christ. Hell in our sense came to be at the same time, for its deepest pain is the loss of heaven, and one could not lose heaven before it existed.

We must think of this article of the Creed, therefore, as saying that Christ died, suffered the hopelessness and dead-endness of death, and yet came through. The "preaching to the dead" that St. Peter talks of will then be the revelation, for the first time, that death was not the end of everything. A heaven had been created beyond death into which all those who had died before Christ could now come for the first time. Of course, there was also created at the same time a hell more terrible than the mere "hell of death," into which the unjust of the time before Christ could now enter.

The medieval theologians, wrestling with these ideas, deduced a state called "limbo," to which they thought the Old Testament just men must have gone; it was a sort of anteroom of the real hell to which the unjust had departed. But we should rather think of "limbo" as the one Old Testament hell, namely, death itself, to which all, just or unjust, descended. Only with the coming of Christ was a new life offered to the dead, and limbo transformed at Christ's resurrection into either heaven or hell.

What is meant by the words "the third day he rose again from the dead"?

By the words "the third day he rose again from the dead" is meant that after Christ had been dead and buried for almost three days he raised his blessed body to life on the third day.

On what day did Christ rise again from the dead?

Christ rose again from the dead on Easter Sunday.

Christ's resurrection is nothing less than the creation of heaven, the opening of the way for us to share the eternal life of the Father. It is in a real sense, therefore, the most important article of the Creed, and we must meditate upon it as deeply as we can.

Perhaps we could begin by giving the *wrong* reason for Christ's resurrection appearing in the Creed. It is not just there as the greatest of Christ's miracles, proving that he was God. When one treats the resurrection like that, one treats it as an historical fact that anyone could have observed if he had been there at the time, or that can now be proven to have been an historical fact; and the clear historical fact is used to justify a more mysterious statement about Christ—that he was God.

But the resurrection is included in the Creed, not as something anyone could *see*, but as something in which to *believe*. It is not what was clear about it that is really important, but its mysterious quality, its deep meaning. To understand all this we must go back a bit.

Since we announced, in the second article, that we pledged our faith to our Lord Jesus Christ, we have been talking about Jesus and trying to plumb the mystery of him. We have turned our attention largely to his bodily life, in which he is our brother, our flesh and blood (as we say). He was conceived, born, suffered, was crucified, died, and was buried, descended into hell—all because he shared our flesh and blood which is subject to suffering and death.

But now we start to see this bodily relationship with other men not so much as we pulling Christ down to death with us, as he pulling us up to life with him. In the resurrection, the ascension, the sending of the Holy Spirit, we shall be seeing his bodily life, now become glorious and eternal, as the source of all our future life.

In the last few pages we saw that the death of Christ was an act of infinite love, which is nothing else than the life of God. The dying of Christ in his human body was the clearest possible manifestation of his divine life. Perhaps we could say that on Calvary the eternal life of God was incarnated in Christ's human death. For the first time in human history, death became a source of life. This is symbolized by the flowing of the water of the Spirit from Christ's side after his death, that water in which the Church is baptized and comes to birth, and in which, through the Church, sprung from Christ, the whole world is to be renewed. Eternal life broke through into the world on Calvary under the form of death.

We can draw an inadequate parallel to what happened if we think of a man like President Kennedy, and the Peace Corps that he founded—that organization of young Americans who volunteer to go out all over the world and work for the good of underdeveloped countries. One can say that although Kennedy is dead, his spirit lives on in the Peace Corps. So also Christ died, but his Spirit lives on in the Church. Only there is this difference. We say that Kennedy personally is dead, and it is the Peace Corps that keeps him alive. But we say that Christ personally is alive, and that it is he who keeps his Church from dying.

The unbeliever does not see this difference. He sees only that Christ has died, and that a human organization at least tries to keep him alive in spirit. But the believer, with only the same human facts to go on, sees a different meaning in them, indeed sees the whole thing completely the other way up. It is not the Church which keeps Christ alive, but Christ who keeps the Church alive. In all the ways in which the Church remembers Christ (we call them the "sacraments"), the believer sees not so much us preserving Christ, as Christ preserving us.

Another way to state this truth is to say that Kennedy will stay alive only as long as his Peace Corps lives, certainly only as long as the world exists. But Christ at his death entered into an eternal life, which will outlast the world, and will carry those people who follow Christ into eternal life with him when the world ends.

Here is the full mysterious meaning of the resurrection. We are believing that the death of Christ did not kill him; rather, he killed death. He has become the Lord of life. When the whole world ceases to exist, Christ's life will live on, and we who have joined ourselves to it in this world (by dying with him) will live on with him.

What is the sixth article of the Creed?

The sixth article of the Creed is, "he ascended into heaven, and sits at the right hand of God, the Father almighty."

What is meant by the words "he ascended into heaven"?

By the words "he ascended into heaven" is meant that our Saviour went up body and soul into heaven on ascension day, forty days after his resurrection.

What is meant by the words "and sits at the right hand of God, the Father almighty"?

The words "and sits at the right hand of God, the Father almighty" do not mean that God the Father has hands, for he is a spirit; but that Christ as God is equal to the Father, and as man is in the highest place in heaven.

In recent years there has been a great movement towards what is called the "demythologization" of the Bible, that is to say, expressing in other language (more intelligible to modern man) what the Scriptures express in "mythological" or "picturesque" terms. The trouble, of course, is that some people throw away the baby with the bath water—in getting rid of the "mythical picture" they get rid of the things essential to the faith, too.

But if we avoid such extremes, "demythologization" is a very necessary activity and not an especially new one. Indeed, the catechism does it in the few questions above, when it says that we must not take "the right hand of God the Father almighty" literally, for God does not really have hands; we only "picture" him as having hands. It might have gone further and said that heaven is not really "up," though we picture it as "up," and thus the very phrase "ascended into heaven" is something we should not take too literally.

When we say that heaven is not up we are not necessarily denying that forty days after his resurrection our Lord appeared for the last time, and left his disciples by being lifted up from the earth into a cloud. But we are saying that our Lord chose to disappear in this way, not because it was the *way* to heaven, but because it *symbolized* for us the way to heaven.

All the resurrection appearances have this element of symbolism in them. Thus our Lord really appeared in bodily form, and ate and drank and talked of peace with his disciples; but these real appearances at the same time symbolized a much deeper reality. The gatherings with his disciples were a forty-day symbol for the everlasting presence of our Lord in the gatherings of the Church. His eating and drinking with them were symbols of the common meal which has been the feature of gatherings of Christ's Church ever since. The peace was the peace of reconciliation of mankind with God.

Even further, all these appearances were symbolizing the future presence of Christ to mankind in heaven for all eternity, at the great banquet of the heavenly marriage feast. When Christ considered that he had sufficiently symbolized the reality that was to last forever, he brought the appearances to a close—by ascending into the cloud that throughout the Bible is a "picture" of God's eternal glory.

Now, of course, Christ has been in the glory of God from the moment of his resurrection, so that what he symbolized in this way forty days after Easter had in fact been true ever since Easter. Indeed, it is only in Luke that the "ascension" of Jesus is dated in this way. In St. John's Gospel, Christ ascends on Easter Sunday between seeing Mary Magdalene (who is not allowed to touch him because he has not yet ascended) and the apostles (who *are* positively urged to touch him).

For it was the resurrection that was the true entry into glory, the entry into eternal life. From that moment onward, Christ, even in his human flesh and blood, was Lord of life and conqueror of death.

This is what is symbolized by the sitting at the right hand of the Father. This is a full share of eternal life with the Father—the right hand representing the place of greatest honor, and the sitting showing us that Christ is no longer there as a servant but as sharing the lordship of God.

The same thing is being taught in all these articles of the Creed—from the suffering under Pontius Pilate to the sitting at the right hand of the Father—as is taught in the following passage from St. Paul's epistle to the Philippians.

"His state was divine, yet he did not cling to his equality with God but emptied himself to assume the condition of a slave, and became as men are; and being as all men are, he was humbler yet, even to accepting death, death on a cross. But God raised him on high and gave him the name which is above all other names, so that all beings in the heavens, on earth, and in the underworld should bend the knee at the name of Jesus, and that every tongue should acclaim Jesus Christ as Lord, to the glory of God the Father."

What is the seventh article of the Creed?

The seventh article of the Creed is, "from thence he shall come to judge the living and the dead."

When will Christ come again?

Christ will come again from heaven at the last day, to judge all mankind.

What are the things Christ will judge?

Christ will judge our thoughts, words, works, and omissions.

What will Christ say to the wicked?

Christ will say to the wicked, "Depart from me, you cursed ones, into the everlasting fire which was prepared for the devil and his angels."

What will Christ say to the just?

Christ will say to the just, "Come, you blessed of my Father, and possess the kingdom prepared for you."

Will everyone be judged at death, as well as at the last day?

Everyone will be judged at death as well as at the last day: "It is appointed unto man once to die, and after this the judgment."

What the catechism here calls the seventh article of the Creed is the final part of what we have called the second article: "I believe in Jesus Christ." We have seen that the whole Creed is a proclamation of our fidelity to God: Father, Son, and Spirit. First of all, in the first article of the Creed, we proclaimed our belief in God the Father almighty who created us and is the source of our being and of all good things. But we can only pledge ourselves

103

to him because we have met him in his Son. He, so to speak, reproduced himself in the form of the man Jesus Christ, who was, in human form, that eternal response to the Father that we call his Son. Thus from the so-called second article of the Creed down to the one we are now considering, we have been proclaiming our faith in that Son.

We have recognized the Father giving himself to us in the becoming flesh of the Son, and his suffering and dying for us on the cross. We have also recognized the gift of divine life given to us through that death, and through the resurrection and ascension which followed it: the gift of loving the Father as the Son loves the Father, of ourselves responding to the Father as he does. But in us this response is not complete; only when the whole of mankind and the whole of the world has become one with Christ in his love of the Father will we be able to talk of that response as complete. Then the Son will have become present in us in a new way: not simply as one man among many, but now present in the whole of mankind. This situation we still look forward to, and it is part of what we mean when we talk of a second coming of Christ, a second presence of the Son in the world. It is this second coming that is the subject of the so-called seventh article of the Creed, the last phrase of what we have called the second article—our proclamation of belief in Jesus Christ.

In this article the second coming is referred to, however, as a coming in judgment. What can this mean? When Christ was living on this earth he said, "God sent his Son into the world not to judge the world, but so that through him the world might be saved." Christ came to bring life and light and love to mankind, not to bring further death and darkness and hatred.

But Christ went on to say that even life and light and love

104

can become a judgment on those who do not accept it. "No one who believes in him will be judged; but whoever refuses to believe is already judged, just because he has refused to believe. . . . Though the light has come into the world, men have shown they prefer darkness to the light. . . . Everyone who does wrong hates the light and avoids it for fear his actions should be exposed; only the man who lives by the truth comes out into the light so that it may be plainly seen that what he does is done in God."

So we can draw several conclusions. In one sense, *Christ does not judge us at all,* we judge ourselves by accepting or not accepting the light and life that is offered to us. But in another sense, *it is precisely the life of Christ that is our judge;* that is the touchstone by which we are judged; it is by a comparison with that life that our life will be seen to be light or darkness.

Again, in one sense, *this judgment is already going on,* for we are already living in the last day. Every time we choose wrongly we move away from the light, every time we humbly give ourselves up to truth, we move towards the light; and this is what the judgment is—to be separated into light or darkness, the right hand or the left, the sheep or the goats. We are doing it to ourselves at every moment.

In this sense, the second coming of our Lord is already taking place in the world. To the precise degree to which we allow him in, he is coming as our eternal king; if we do not allow him in, he is still coming, but as judge. This is what our Lord meant when the night before he died he said to the high priests, "From this time onward you will see the Son of man seated on the right hand of the power of God and coming on the clouds of heaven."

But, in another sense, *the judgment will finally come on us only when we die.* For it is part of the meaning of dying that it puts an end to our shuffling between light and darkness and freezes us in whatever state we have reached. We are judging ourselves all our life; that judgment will come home to roost at death.

The same is true of the world and the human race as a whole. Just as there comes a time for each man to die, and after that (or better, perhaps, in that very moment) his judgment comes upon him, so too there will come a time for the whole world and mankind to die, and in that very moment the whole race of mankind will find itself judged by what it itself has chosen.

The early Christians seem to have thought that the day of judgment was very near; and from time to time people arise who claim to know its time. We have no reason to think that God is going to do something especially disastrous to the world "out of the blue," so to speak; rather, it seems that he will leave the world to destroy itself. Thus our modern tendency to put the day off and think of it as remote is quite possibly true, and sermons which pretend it might come tomorrow do not usually carry much conviction.

But what *is* terribly true, and we should remind ourselves of it each day, is that in another sense the day of judgment is going on all the time. Every day in every one of our actions we are judging ourselves, doing irrevocable things which displace us either to the left or the right, either into darkness or into light. There is a real truth in the claim that the day of judgment is actually upon us. At our own death our own personal judgment will come home to roost on us. Just because Christ is the full and infinite mercy of God, anyone who rejects him is totally and without recall condemned to death.

When this judgment is complete, the world will finally have ranged itself with or against Christ, and those who have ranged

106

themselves with him will have become part of that total and complete response to the Father towards which he has been working throughout history. The Father will have drawn his Son out of this world of ours in the fullest sense. We live in the period between the first coming of the Son and the second; we live in the period when the world is joining itself to or disjoining itself from Jesus. It is a period which can very specially be described as the period of God's presence in the world through his Holy Spirit, as we shall see in turning now to consider the third and final part of the Creed: "I believe in the Holy Spirit."

PART THREE

THE HOLY SPIRIT

Both Father and Son are equally God, they are one in nature. Only in this do they differ, that one is God as fathering, and the other God as being fathered; they differ, we say, as persons. And yet, in their very difference from one another, they embrace one another in a new kind of unity—the kind of unity that is possible between different persons, a community of love. God, so to speak, is not merely a unity of nature underlying these two persons, but he is a unity actively breathed forth from the two of them, their common Spirit or Breath, namely, God the Holy Spirit.

What is the eighth article of the Creed?

The eighth article of the Creed is, "I believe in the Holy Spirit."

Who is the Holy Spirit?

The Holy Spirit is the third person of the Blessed Trinity.

From whom does the Holy Spirit proceed?

The Holy Spirit proceeds from the Father and the Son.

Is the Holy Spirit equal to the Father and to the Son?

The Holy Spirit is equal to the Father and to the Son, for he is the same Lord and God as they are.

Just as we express our thoughts in words, so we express our love in gifts. The word stands between person and person as a means of communicating their thoughts to one another; the gift stands between person and person as a means of communicating their love to one another.

If the eternal Son is called the Word of the Father, it is because he expresses, represents, reproduces the Father to himself. God, in knowing himself, expresses himself, speaks himself out; as speaking we call him God the Father, as spoken we call him God the Son or God the Word.

If we now think of the unity of these two persons as a unity of love, a unity breathed forth by both, then there is no better word perhaps in our languages for God the Holy Spirit than to call him the Gift. God the Holy Spirit is the mutual gift of Father and Son, and what they give each other is equally God with them.

But in Jesus Christ, the Father has spoken himself in human

form, the Son has become incarnate; and in the Son's death, resurrection, and ascension we have seen the Son's return of love to his Father. That is why we read that on the cross and at his resurrection God the Spirit was breathed forth in this human world of ours. The eternal breathing forth of the Spirit became a human fact; the man, who was the Son of God, breathed him forth to his Father within this world.

But, as we have seen, this is not the final presence of the Son in this world of ours; that is yet to come at the second coming of Christ when the whole redeemed mankind will be gathered together into the Son, and therefore gathered together with Christ into the breathing forth of the Spirit to the Father. That this will happen is already guaranteed to the world by the breathing forth on Calvary and at the resurrection and at Pentecost. The Holy Spirit now dwells in the world, God as gift, the pledge of the final incorporation of the world into the life of the Trinity at the last day. He dwells in the world already as breathed forth by Christ, he dwells in us already insofar as we are joined to Christ in faith and help breathe him forth to God and to one another, and he will dwell finally and totally with us when we are joined to Christ for all eternity, no longer in faith and hope, but in face-to-face vision. In the meantime, we can think of the Holy Spirit in us as the presence of the risen Christ in us breathing forth love for his Father. For Christ has not only risen in his own body into heaven, but is rising, so to speak, in us until the last day of our resurrection and glorification.

The last article of the Creed proclaims our belief in this Gift within us, proclaims our fidelity to the wind of God blowing in us from the resurrection. Perhaps we can think of it as the wind that Christ's passing to heaven has left in its wake, and which is gathering us up to follow him.

This belief in God present as Gift within us is expressed by the Creed in a whole catalogue of phrases. Because this Gift is the presence of Father and Son in *spirit* within us we proclaim our belief in the Holy Spirit. Because this Gift welds us into a universal *community of grace gathered around Christ* we proclaim our belief in the holy catholic Church, the communion of saints; for "catholic" here is the Greek for "universal," and "Church" translates the Greek word for a "gathering."

Because this Gift breaks down the barriers between us and God we proclaim our belief in *the forgiveness of sin;* because it takes up even our bodily life into God's glory we proclaim our belief in *the resurrection of the body;* and because it is in fact the Gift of God's own life we proclaim our belief in that *everlasting Life*.

We begin by saying, "I believe in the Holy Spirit." The word *spirit* is derived from the Lation word for "wind"; and perhaps the image we should have in our minds is that last breath of Jesus on the cross with which, as he died, he breathed forth life on the world. From that moment a wind of love, God's love for men, is blowing through the world. Jesus himself breathed it into his disciples on Easter Sunday, saying, "Receive the Holy Spirit." On Pentecost Sunday it escaped into the whole earth with a sound like that of a mighty wind. Or, as we said, we can think of it as the wind left by Christ in his journey to the Father.

Is this not a fine image for our whole Christian life? We are like birds who need a wind to soar on, and at the same time, by soaring on the invisible wind, make it visible to the world. The Spirit blows through our hearts—the Spirit of Jesus' love blowing from Calvary—and we by responding to it, by allowing ourselves to be blown by it, make it present to everyone else.

But then we must add that *this* wind does not exist for the sake of the birds, but we birds exist for the sake of the wind. This wind existed long before we birds; it has always existed in the eternal nature of God and we were created to be temporal recipients of it. For God's love is not like our love, called into existence by the things we find lovable: God's love creates things for him to love. So it is that the wind in us is the same Spirit that Father and Son have been breathing forth from all eternity. The Holy Spirit given to us on Calvary is the eternal mutual gift of Father and Son, as much God as they themselves are.

THE CHURCH

When did the Holy Spirit come down on the apostles?

The Holy Spirit came down on the apostles on Pentecost Sunday, in the form of "parted tongues, as it were, of fire."

Why did the Holy Spirit come down on the apostles?

The Holy Spirit came down on the apostles to confirm their faith, to sanctify them, and to enable them to found the Church.

The Holy Spirit is that holy wind of God which breathes in us now from the cross. For Christ has not only risen into heaven, but has risen, so to speak, into us; and the Spirit of Christ and of his Father is in us, continually drawing us towards resurrection.

If sin can be thought of as the force of Adam within us pulling us towards death, then the Spirit is the force of Christ within us pulling us towards resurrection.

We usually put it this way: the Father, we say, sent his only Son into the world—that is to say, sent him to us as the gift to us of himself. We say also that the Father, in and through his Son, sent his Spirit into the world—that is to say, the sending of the Son has now become the sending of all who follow him. We also have become the gift of God to the world; the Spirit of God and of Christ lives in us, their breath breathes in us.

That is why the notions of the Spirit and of the apostles are so closely connected in our Christian faith. *Apostle* is the Greek word for "one who is sent." We are all apostles of the Father and of Christ because their Spirit breathes in us and blows us onward, and we in turn breathe it forth to others. The Spirit that thus inspires us is the Spirit of God's truth and love and holiness; it is the gift of God's own way of living.

But there is also a special band of people to whom the name *apostle* particularly applies. That is because the process of God giving himself, of the Father sending his Son and his Spirit, is an historical process. Historically speaking, Christ began the process by sending certain people, who sent others, who sent others, and so on down to ourselves in the present day, who must ourselves send others to future generations. The very first people to be sent bý Christ we call, very specially, *the* apostles.

This is the significance of the coming down of the Spirit on the apostles on Pentecost Sunday. They were to be the visible beginnings of the long process of *sending* (which we call the Church). The sending of God, the wind of God, came down upon them therefore in a special visible way. In them the gathering of the people of God to resurrection began that process which was to halt and reverse the scattering due to sin. Thus, just as at Babel sin had manifested itself in scattered languages (one might say dispersed tongues) and the confusion of people into uncommunicating groups, so on Pentecost Sunday the Spirit manifested itself in a collecting together again of the dispersed tongues, and a new confusion of people at finding they could once more communicate.

The Holy Spirit, then, produces the Church and the Church has an historical structure, given it by the Holy Spirit. First, there was Christ, Lord of the Church. Then there was the "apostolic age" upon which all succeeding ages depend for their sending, and to which they must always return for confirmation of their

116

faith and refreshment in grace. Then there is the age of the present world on pilgrimage to the final age to come, being *sent* by God towards resurrection and towards the new heaven and new earth.

As a result of this historical structure the Church has an institutional structure, also given it by the Holy Spirit. For, in the age of the present world, certain members of the Church have it as their special duty to represent for us the "apostolic age," to be for us today channels through which God sends us. These are the bishops, the representatives of the first apostles. The truth and love and holiness of the Father, revealed to us in Jesus Christ his Son, and now given to us in the Holy Spirit, come to us through the faith and sacraments of the "apostolic age" handed on to us through our present bishops.

What is the ninth article of the Creed?

The ninth article of the Creed is "the holy catholic Church, the communion of saints."

What is the catholic Church?

The catholic Church is the union of all the faithful under one head.

Who is the head of the catholic Church?

The head of the catholic Church is Jesus Christ our Lord.

The final articles of the Creed are expansions of the eighth article, expressing more fully our faith in the Holy Spirit, that wind of God which is blowing through the world from the cross, breathing forth "forgiveness of sins" (tenth article) and gathering us with Christ to "resurrection of the body" (eleventh article) and "life everlasting" (twelfth article). This separation of men from sin and gathering of them to Christ by the Spirit is called "the holy catholic Church, the communion of saints" (ninth article).

The catechism approaches the Church in the following way. It describes her first of all as the gathering of the faithful round their Lord (three questions), then discusses her visible and hierarchical structure (eight questions), turns next to some of her characteristic qualities, including holiness and inerrancy (eight questions), and finally talks of the communion between her earthly and heavenly members (three questions). An appendix on purgatory is added.

Now it is in this matter of our approach to the Church that the recent Council has most profoundly affected Catholic thinking. Yet the basic pattern followed by the catechism is also followed in the *Constitution on the Church*.

This document starts with seventeen paragraphs on the mystery of the Church as the gathering of the people of God. Much more stress is laid on this fact in the Council decree than in the catechism, but in both it is the first thing treated.

The Council goes on to twenty-one paragraphs on the Church's hierarchical structure and the role of the laity. Again the pattern is the same as that of the catechism, but a new emphasis is brought in, for the catechism treats mainly of the Pope, while the Council stresses also the roles of bishops and laity.

The next nine paragraphs of the Council document deal with the call of the Church to holiness, both laity and religious. Here again a parallel can be drawn with the catechism, but the special stress on holiness is marked, and on holiness as a call rather than as an achieved state of affairs.

Finally, the Council document has three paragraphs relating the Church on earth to the Church in heaven (compare again the catechism), but the stress is laid on the "incomplete" pilgrim nature of the earthly Church. The Council document also adds an appendix on Mary and her role in the Church.

So here we have a very good example of what this book is all about. The expression and emphasis given to Catholic doctrines change as the Church develops: but the basic truths which are being expressed and emphasized remain the same basic truths they always were. The new stress in talking of the Church is on the gathering of a people together in *response* to the call of God: a developing, historical process which will never be completely

119

achieved till the end of the world. The old stress was on the abiding grace of the call itself, already present in the Church, and expressing itself through her solid and permanent structures.

But we can integrate both ways of seeing the Church. If we stress the word *faithful* in the catechism's definition of the Church—"the union of all the faithful under one head"—then we see that for the catechism also the Church is a gathering of men in *response* to God's loving call. For (as we have earlier said) "faith" is not just an assent to certain dogmas, but a personal putting of our faith in him who loves us. The Church is men responding to the call of the Spirit and gathering round the one Lord.

In this connection it would be interesting to know if the answer to the third catechism question above surprised anyone who read it. Did anyone expect the answer to be "The head of the Catholic Church is the Pope"? If so, perhaps that would illustrate why the Church has felt it necessary to shift emphasis away from ecclesiastical structures, and stress instead the deep mystery of which these structures are the external and sacramental signs. It is true that the Pope is in a special way our shepherd, teacher, and father (as the catechism will later say): but this is because he represents in a special way our one king (in Hebrew the same word as shepherd), our one prophet and teacher, our one priestly father, namely, Jesus Christ our Lord.

The Church, then, is a mysterious gathering of responding people around the call of him whom the Council names our King, Prophet, and Priest. Just as he embodied the life of God in the form of God's Word calling to us, so the Church embodies the same divine life in the form of a response to the Word, a body answering to its head. The Church is the wife of the Lord, joining herself in mysterious marriage vows to her divine Husband.

Has the Church a visible head on earth?

The Church has a visible head on earth—the bishop of Rome, who is the vicar of Christ.

Why is the bishop of Rome the head of the Church?

The bishop of Rome is the head of the Church because he is the successor of St. Peter, whom Christ appointed to be the head of the Church.

How do we know that Christ appointed St. Peter to be head of the Church?

We know that Christ appointed St. Peter to be head of the Church because Christ said to him, "Thou art Peter, and upon this rock I will build my Church, and the gates of hell shall not prevail against it. And to thee I will give the keys of the kingdom of heaven."

We have already said that it is in our approach to the Church that Vatican Council II has most profoundly affected Catholic thinking. The basic truths about the Church remain, of course, unaltered, but the stress has been changed.

The catechism, for instance, has defined the Church as the union of faithful under their one head, Jesus Christ; the new stress in the Council brings out the fact that "faithful" means people who are responding to a call, and that the Church is to be thought of as a developing, historical gathering of people together in a gradually growing response to God's love.

The Council goes on to talk of the people who make this response: the laity organized into a visible society with their bishops and priests. Then it deals with the call itself from God ever present to these people: the call to holiness present in the sacraments and the Mass. Finally, it deals with the completed Church which will be attained only in heaven.

Now the catechism pattern is the same, but the stress is different. The catechism also begins with the visible structure of the Church, but it lays far more stress on the high point of this structure—the papacy—than it does on the structure of laity, priests, and bishops as a whole.

Perhaps it should be our duty, in commenting on the catechism, to bring out how the papacy fits into this structure, rather than to stress its isolation from the rest of the Church. We have already prepared the ground in a way by talking earlier about the historical structure of the Church, given to it by the Holy Spirit. The Spirit is the wind of Christ blowing through the world; but it would not be visible to the world unless people responded to it; no more than the wind of nature would be visible to us unless trees and birds and scraps of paper responded to it and showed it to us.

Now the first people to respond to this mighty wind were the apostles at Pentecost; it became visible for the first time in them. Only because they responded to it have succeeding ages been able to feel the wind and respond to it themselves. So the Church has a definite historical structure; its response to God's call has a structure: first, the apostolic age; then the intervening ages including our own; and finally, the last and perfect age still to come when the Church will be completed in heaven.

Because the Church has this historical structure it also has an institutional structure. In any age there are certain members who have it as their special duty to represent for us the "apostolic age," to be for us the channels of the wind of the Spirit, to be the first and most visible responders to this wind. Such are the bishops. Trying to express their role we call them "the successors of the apostles." This does not mean that the bishops replace the apostles, taking over every duty in the Church that the apostles had. As we read in the preface said on apostles' feasts, the apostles are still in charge of the Church, still leading its response—they are still the foundation stones of the Church and nobody can replace them.

Rather, we mean that the bishops are those people in our own age who "represent" in a visible manner and remind us of this irreplaceable place of the apostles. They "stand for" the apostles who themselves have become invisible to us.

Thus, just as the apostles themselves grouped themselves around Peter, without any diminution of their own authority, so the bishops are grouped around one of their number—called significantly in the catechism the *bishop* of Rome—without any diminution of the God-given authority of bishops. For Christ said to Peter, "The devil desired to own you apostles and sift you as wheat, but I have prayed for you, Peter, that you not fail in faith, and then you could turn and be a source of strength to the other apostles, your brethren."

In a similar sort of way one bishop among the rest represents this special strength that Christ has given to his apostles. The bishops as a whole stand for (are the vicars of) the apostolic age; one among them stands in a special way for their Christ-given strength to fail not.

But all the bishops are, of course, servants of the Church as a whole. They are there to help strengthen the response of the whole people of God to the call of the Spirit, and to help gather them around Christ.

What is the bishop of Rome called?

The bishop of Rome is called the Pope; this word signifies "father."

Is the Pope the spiritual father of all Christians?

The Pope is the spiritual father of all Christians.

Is the Pope the shepherd and teacher of all Christians?

The Pope is the shepherd and teacher of all Christians, because Christ made St. Peter the shepherd of the whole flock when he said, "Feed my lambs, feed my sheep." He also prayed that his faith might never fail, and commanded him to confirm his brethren.

Is the Pope infallible?

The Pope is infallible.

What is meant by saying that the Pope is infallible?

When it is said that the Pope is infallible, what is meant is that the Pope cannot err when, as shepherd and teacher of all Christians, he defines a doctrine concerning faith or morals, to be held by the whole Church.

The questions above deal exclusively with one member of the Church—the Pope; they have nothing to say about the other bishops, or about all the rest of the baptized people of God. It is as though somebody discussing an orchestra were to speak exclusively about the first violinist.

For the Church, in many ways, is like that orchestra which gave a memorial concert for its recently dead conductor; and did it on that night without a conductor, thus showing how deeply

124

the spirit of the conductor had entered into each member of the orchestra. The church is a gathering of those in whose hearts the spirit of Jesus still lives, and who gather especially in their liturgical assemblies to remember him.

Christ is the Church's conductor: her king, priest, and prophet. The members of the Church are his followers, and the principal members of the Church are those who lead her in that following: first of all, the apostles, and then our present bishops whose special office it is to represent the apostles to us; and these bishops can be compared with the leaders of the various sections of an orchestra.

Among them the one who represents the apostle Peter is of special importance. He is in a special manner our father, leading us in response to Christ our Priest; our shepherd, leading us in response to Christ our King; our teacher, leading us in response to Christ our Prophet. We have compared him with the leader of the violins who is also the leader of the whole orchestra; a bishop among bishops who is also leader of the whole Church.

Christ has promised us that—as long as we are humble and sensitive to his Spirit within us—our following of him will not fail, will be infallible. Each of us must listen first and foremost to the Spirit within our hearts. We cannot live a properly Christian life simply by waiting without thought or love for others to tell us what to do. The music must be in us. However, the Spirit is a spirit of following our leaders—the apostles and their representatives; and the promise that *we* shall be infallible includes the promise that *they* shall not fail in leading us.

Infallibility does not mean that Pope and bishops will be unfailingly holy or wise; it means rather that God places a guard about them to preserve us from any human wickedness or stupidity that might be in them. Christ chose as the Church's Rock an apostle who was, a few verses later, rebuked for blindness and called Satan; the threefold call to feed the flock went to a man who had denied Christ thrice. It was only Christ's prayer for Peter that gave him the faith not to sink in the waves but to walk the waters.

Indeed, we suggest that the catechism answer "The Pope is infallible" is misleading. It should read, "The Pope *is not* infallible *except* in certain peculiar circumstances."

Popes and bishops have exercised their leadership in many different forms during the centuries. We are emerging at the moment from a period when that exercise of leadership took a very authoritarian form. But it seems that future centuries might see a return to an earlier way such as the first centuries of the Church enjoyed. This must not cause us a crisis of security. Our security rests primarily on the Spirit in the Church, in whatever form it shows itself, whether that be outwardly a great show of authority or not.

We have seen in our own days, in John XXIII, how a Pope can lead the world by example and by inspiration, rather than by rebukes; and how he can succeed by such methods in gathering Christ's "orchestra" to its conductor very much better than would have been possible by authoritarian laying down of the law.

We ought to pray constantly for our bishops that they may worthily fill the offices that have been given to them; if it is their duty to lead us, it is our duty to pray for them, so that the prayer of Christ may still go up to the Father for Peter, and turning he may be able to strengthen his brethren.

Has the Church of Christ any marks by which we might know her?

The Church of Christ has four marks by which we may know her: she is one, she is holy, she is catholic, she is apostolic.

How is the Church one?

The Church is one because all her members agree in one faith, have all the same sacrifice and sacraments, and are all united under one head.

How is the Church holy?

The church is holy because she teaches a holy doctrine, offers to all the means of holiness, and is distinguished by the eminent holiness of so many thousands of her children.

What does the word "catholic" mean?

The word *catholic* means universal.

How is the Church catholic or universal?

The Church is catholic or universal because she subsists in all ages, teaches all nations, and is the one ark of salvation for all.

How is the Church apostolic?

The Church is apostolic because she holds the doctrines and traditons of the apostles, and because, through the unbroken succession of her pastors, she derives her orders and her mission from them.

The catechism has defined the Church as the union of all the faithful under one head, Jesus Christ our Lord. So far we have been laying the stress on the faithful: the people of God gathering around Christ and responding to his call with their faith. We have talked of the laity, of the bishops, of the Pope; all of them are members of the faithful acknowledging Christ as Lord.

Thus we suggested that the Church is like an orchestra, giving a memorial concert to its great conductor after his death; he has gone away in the flesh and the conducting dais is empty, but his spirit has so entered into the orchestra members that they can go on playing the music he taught them.

But if we were to think of the Church as simply like an orchestra—a gathering of musicians responding to the lead of the conductor—our emphasis would remain a little Protestant. For it is the Protestant tradition that has stressed the Church as a "congregation" of men, fragile and finite. In the past few years we Catholics have been discovering how much truth there is in this emphasis, and making room in our concept of the Church for the notions of human failure and, even, sin. But this emphasis must be balanced with the concept of the Church as Christ himself among us: a concept which has always been present in Catholic tradition. The "congregation" of the faithful is also the body of Christ: an organism in which he still lives in spirit. In terms of our analogy we must remember that this orchestra is filled with the music of Christ, with the music of God. For this is one way of looking at the Holy Spirit: he is the eternal music that Father and Son make together, and this music now belongs forever to the Church.

The music is there, but it will not be heard by the audience of mankind unless the Church plays it. The holy wind of God will not be visible to men unless the members of the Church, like birds, fly on it, dipping and soaring and responding to its impulse. It is to this aspect of the Church that the catechism is now turning, when it asks about the distinguishing marks of the Church of Christ.

In the last analysis what distinguishes the Church is its divine music, but this becomes audible to the world only when its members play it properly. So it is that the catechism talks of the unity of the Church as something already possessed: the music of its faith, the Mass, and the sacraments, all derived from the one conductor and head, Jesus Christ. But, of course, because of sin and human failure, the true extent of this unity is not visible to the world in our days, and it is for this reason that the Council has laid such stress on ecumenism and the healing of all schism in the Church.

Again, holiness belongs to the Church in principle, in her doctrine and sacraments, but the world sees not only the many thousands who have become holy in her, but also the many thousands who have not.

The Church is universal, designed for all men in all ages and in all parts of the globe; but because of human failure and of sin in her members she often appears narrow and limited to one sort of culture. So again the Council lays great stress on the need for the Church to be greater than, say, white civilization or Western culture.

Finally, the Church is apostolic, deriving from the apostles in whom Christ first embodied his spirit; but that apostolicity must be seen in action, her mission must be clear to the world. On this last point above all the Council exhorts us to expand the notions of the Church that we have received from the catechism, and to realize that we are called to be the salt of the earth, a leaven in the world, in the forefront of all attempts to create this universe of ours anew in Christ.

Let us now briefly discuss the changing Church, or the Church on the move. Everything that the catechism has to say about the Church assumes that the Church is unchanging and settled.

Nevertheless, we cannot escape today the knowledge that the Church is changing, even if we disapprove. If we are not to be completely confused, we must know where this sort of change fits into God's plan for his Church, and how it is to be reconciled with the picture of the unchanging Church given us in the catechism. Here the recent Vatican Council can help us, with its picture of the Church as a growing Church, a pilgrim Church, and a leaven in the midst of the world.

First of all, the Church is a *growing* Church. It is like any other growing thing, in that it preserves its own settled identity and yet develops in maturity and self-knowledge. We human beings are like that: indeed *must* be like that, if we are not to degenerate. A person in a state of arrested development ceases to be fully human. That is the way God made us.

That is also the way he made his Church. She is not just a flock, but a vineyard; not just a temple, but a mother; she is living, and therefore growing. We have called her an "orchestra," but just as the orchestra has developed during the ages, improving the number and quality of its instruments, exploring new forms of melody, harmony, and rhythm, so also the Church has developed both institutionally and in her appreciation of the richness implicit in her doctrine and tradition.

This is one of the reasons why St. Paul talked of the Church as Christ's body; for "if we live by the truth and in love, we shall grow in all ways into Christ, who is the head by whom the whole body is fitted and joined together, every joint adding its own strength, for each separate part to work according to its function. So the body grows until it has built itself up in love."

Now this growing is also a sort of exploring. The Church is a *journeying* Church, on route for a distant goal across difficult country. She is unchanging in this sense: that she is on an unchanging journey to an unchanging goal; but the landscape through which she journeys is forever changing and requiring adaptation from her. Though she must always remain adapted to her goal, she must also discover a path to the goal in all sorts of country, and then be adapted to the road along which she must travel if she is to survive the journey. One of the promises made to the Church by Christ is that she is going to survive the journey, so it must be implied that he is going to be with her in all those necessary adaptations to the road so that she never fails on the way.

The Church, then, is a pilgrim Church, like the Jews in the desert on the way to the promised land; and therefore she is beset by two kinds of dangers: that her eyes would be so much set on the road immediately before her that she might forget her goal, and that her eyes would be so rigidly set on the goal that she might stumble over something directly in her path. Christ will be with her to rescue her from both dangers, and it is part of our faith in him to help the Church journey well.

Finally, this pilgrimage of hers through the world to a goal that is beyond this world makes of her a "leaven" in the midst of the world, a sort of "soul" for the world, as the Council puts it. The Church is not just for Catholics. She is for all men a sign, even if they are not full members of her. Though her goal is not within this world, yet she must be a mother to all those she meets in this world. She must not only be on the move herself, but she must take part in the whole movement of the world, stimulate the rest of mankind to movement, and help them find the path. She is therefore not only a flock which men can be members of in this world, but she points out a way, so that there will be many who will join her for the first time in heaven.

Now these truths about the Church are not to be found in the catechism. This also is part of the growth of the Church. There have been centuries during which the Church was still making explicit what she believed about Christ; then it was time to go on and make explicit what she believed about the Trinity. Later still she made explicit her doctrine about the life of God in men: grace, first, and later, at the time of the Reformation, faith and the sacraments.

In our own days the time has come for a fuller explication of the social nature of the Church, for making explicit the very notion of Church itself. We must live through these times with the same faith and hope that orthodox Christians showed in earlier centuries when other doctrines were developing.

Can the Church err in what she teaches?

The Church cannot err in what she teaches as to faith or morals, for she is our infallible guide in both.

How do we know that the Church cannot err in what she teaches?

We know that the Church cannot err in what she teaches because Christ promised that the gates of hell shall never prevail against his Church (Mt. 16, 18); that the Holy Spirit will teach her all things (Jn. 14, 16–26); and that he himself will be with her all days, even to the consummation of the world (Mt. 28, 20).

By now we are used to the catechism approach which sees the Church first and foremost as a teaching establishment. So it should not surprise us that it phrases its questions about the infallibility of the Church in terms of whether she can err in what she *teaches*, rather than in the wider and more scriptural terms of whether she can err in what she *believes*. Even this distinction perhaps does not break altogether with the image of the Church as one big classroom.

Better is the image of the Church as a band of pilgrims on the move under Christ's leadership to a heavenly kingdom, and the question is: Can she err from the true path, can she be wrongly guided and lose her way? Or, using the image of an orchestra under Christ's conductorship, can she cease to be able to make music, can she produce discord rather than harmony?

Thus the quotations from Scripture given in the catechism

do not primarily guarantee that the Church will be the treasure-house of all speculative truth, but rather that it will succeed in coming to heaven and avoiding hell; that it will be led to the true God by the Spirit; that Christ will be with her as she proceeds on pilgrimage to the consummation of the world.

Infallible does not mean first of all that the teaching Church cannot utter falsehood; it means that the whole Church will be inevitably successful in reaching her end. The word *infallible* is used as it is in the phrase "an infallible remedy."

Now we may understand this better if we reflect on what happened to the world in Christ. He, we know, was God made man. We usually think, when we say this, of God as the Creator, the Almighty One, the Beginning of the world come down into his creation. But we can also see God as the ultimate Heaven, the final Harmony, the End of the world come down already into the world on pilgrimage to that heaven. What is present in the world since Christ is not only the conductor but also the music.

The fact that Christ lived and died in our world has out-weighed any sin that may be committed there, has guaranteed that there will be ultimate harmony despite any conceivable discord. For all music is indeed a weaving together of notes which would in themselves be discordant with one another, so that an ultimate harmony rules. And the coming of Christ has guaranteed, so to speak, that the world will now be infallibly musical, ultimately harmonious. Of course, God has guaranteed this end from the beginning in his eternal decrees, but now the harmony is with us—actually being realized, and even partially discernible to the eyes of faith.

That is why the Council says, "The final age of the world has already come upon us. The renovation of the world has been irrevocably decreed, *and in this age is already anticipated in some real way.*" It is, in fact, *the world* that is infallible since the coming of Christ; and this is actually visible—though imperfectly—in that anticipation of the final harmony that we call the Church.

Thus the Council goes on: "The renovation of the world . . . is already anticipated in this age . . . for even now on this earth the Church is marked with a genuine, though imperfect, holiness." It is the world which is infallible, bound inevitably to reach heaven, insofar as it binds itself to Christ's leadership manifested to us through the apostles; insofar as it binds itself to play his music in consort with the leaders of his Church.

Teaching-infallibility is a necessary consequence of this total infallibility. But it can never be divorced from the infallibility with which the Church moves towards her end. Indeed, it is only in the light of the end that the exact content of any infallible statement can become clear. For we shall only be able to see in its fullness what the Church has actually said, when we come to that end. Nobody except the blessed in heaven can know with complete clarity what any infallible statement of the Church has meant. Ecumenical council after ecumenical council can make it gradually clearer and clearer, but for total clarity we shall have to wait for the final ecumenical council in heaven.

What is meant by "the communion of saints"?

By "the communion of saints" is meant that all the members of the Church, in heaven, on earth, and in purgatory, are in communion with each other, as being one body in Jesus Christ.

How are the faithful on earth in communion with each other?

The faithful on earth are in communion with each other by professing the same faith, obeying the same authority, and assisting each other with their prayers and good works.

How are we in communion with the saints in heaven?

We are in communion with the saints in heaven by honoring them as the glorified members of the Church; and also by praying to them and by their praying for us.

How are we in communion with the souls in purgatory?

We are in communion with the souls in purgatory by helping them with our prayers and good works: "It is a holy and wholesome thought to pray for the dead, that they may be loosed from sins."

There are two pictures we might have in mind when we read in the catechism about "the communion of saints," that fellowship of all members of the Church in heaven, on earth, and in purgatory. We might think of a huge gathering of people divided into three separate sections, as, for example, the crowd in a stadium is composed of those in the grandstand, those on open stands, and those on the embankment.

We might think of the Church triumphant as gathered in the grandstand of heaven, the Church militant as out on the open

stands of earth, and the Church suffering in purgatory as condemned to the embankment. That is one picture.

But it is a rather too static picture. We have seen that the
Church is a Church on the move: a growing Church, a journeying Church, a Church on pilgrimage to heaven. Thus we might
change our picture, so that the Church on earth would then be
the runners engaged in the marathon who are expected in the
stadium at any minute, having run their course. The Church in
heaven would be all those people waiting to cheer them as they
enter (as long as we remember that they have also been round
the course and entered the stadium themselves to cheers once
upon a time). The Church in purgatory would then have to be
compared to those runners who have finished the course, but
are still recovering their breath before going to join the cheering
crowds on the stands.

The Church is a communion of saints, a gathering which
takes place primarily in heaven, a gathering of those people
who have run their course and are now cheering in the stadium.
Or better, it is a "gathering" of people *towards* heaven, towards
where Christ our Lord now sits at the right hand of the Father,
in the royal box. If there is a communion between the people on
earth, it is a fellowship which moves towards this perfect communion in heaven. It is a communion which is on the march
and not yet fully achieved.

The communion of saints is not, therefore, something which
is already there complete around us; it is something which we
have to work for. Indeed, this is perhaps the most profound way
of seeing what our life on earth is all about: our life on earth
is our contribution towards creating the communion of saints.

By our daily work in the world, by our prayers, by our
worship in the Church, we are gathering men together into a

community, helping them to know and love one another, so that eventually and for eternity they may enjoy one another's company round God's throne in heaven.

The Mass itself can be understood in this way, too. At the offertory on Sunday we bring to the altar the work we have done during the week, the contribution we have made to the world. There we join it to the work of the other members of the parish; and then, at the beginning of the canon, we join it to the work of the Pope and bishops, to the work of all who we wish specially to remember, to the work of Mary and Joseph and all the saints already in heaven, to the work of the angels mentioned at the end of the preface. Finally, we join it to the work of Christ himself, to his passion, death, resurrection, and ascension.

The Mass is a sort of foretaste of heaven in this regard, for there the work of all the world will be eternally offered to God, and all the saints will rejoice in it and cheer. The image for this joy in the Scripture is the heavenly banquet when all the saints, after their work is completed, will sit down to a festal meal. In the Mass we have a foretaste of that, too: a banquet of that eternal joy which we are supposed to imbibe and then take out into the world again to spread through all men and peoples.

The communion of the saints, then, is something which is happening now, something that we help to prepare and build up among men by spreading among them Christian love and joy. At every Mass we are reminding ourselves of this duty, and, so to speak, reporting back to heaven on how far we have got with the job.

138

What is purgatory?

Purgatory is a place where souls suffer for a time after death on account of their sins.

Which souls go to purgatory?

Those souls go to purgatory that departed this life in venial sin; or that have not fully paid the debt of temporal punishment due to those sins of which the guilt has been forgiven.

What is temporal punishment?

Temporal punishment is punishment which will have an end, either in this world or in the world to come.

How can it be proved that there is a purgatory?

It can be proved that there is a purgatory from the constant teaching of the Church; and from the doctrine of holy Scripture which declares that God will render to every man according to his works; that nothing defiled shall enter heaven; and that some will be saved, yet so as by fire.

These catechism questions are a sort of appendix to what we have been saying about the Church, for not all members of the Church are on earth or in heaven. Some are in purgatory. But what is purgatory?

All men suffer on account of their sins. We sometimes talk of people escaping scot-free, but this only means that they escape *visible* suffering, or the arbitrary penalties which society imposes. However, quite apart from such visible penalties, every sin weakens the sinner as a human being, and cuts him off from true happiness and delight in the world as God has made it. Every sin against another human being deprives a man of the love and fellowship God wants to give him through that human being.

This sort of suffering is *God's* penalty for sin. God who is man's creator has no need of the sort of external arbitrary penalties that society imposes. He has made man in such a way that every sin carries with it its own necessary and interior retribution. Of course, we can compare the interior suffering that sin causes with the external punishment that society imposes; but it is dangerous, for we might end up picturing God as an arbitrary external policeman. Purgatory, for example, is not arbitrary external punishment, but the deep working-out of sin's inherent consequences. It is not a jail, even if it helps sometimes to picture it as a "place" where we suffer for a "time." For, of course, place and time cannot have their usual meanings when they are applied not to bodies but to souls.

We should indeed note the explanation of the word *time* given above by the catechism. It is not that purgatory itself necessarily takes up time; but purgatory is suffering for sin which would normally have been our lot during this temporal life, but in fact had not fully worked itself out when death came along and suddenly put an end to time for us. Every sin requires its period of convalescence, its process of healing, and this we call its "temporal punishment"; but if this is not complete at death, it must be completed "somewhere" and at some other "time."

If death is thought of simply as a moment of transition from one life to another, then we may simply say that, since the healing has not fully come in the life before death, it must come in the life afterwards. This is our normal way of conceiving of purgatory. But perhaps it would be permissible to explore another way of thinking about purgatory, in a way which avoids the very difficult notion of time going on after death. Such an exploration is purely speculative, and only justified if it remains true to the basic teaching of the Church.

One would start by remembering that death is not only the end moment of life, but also the heaviest suffering that any man has to bear. We are not talking about the particular *way* in which a man dies—painfully or not—but simply the *fact* that he has to die. In the moment of dying a man has to take leave of all the created happinesses and pleasures to which he had clung during life; and the closer our sins have enslaved us to those pleasures the more of a punishment death will be.

Now if a man has not sufficiently recovered from his sins before his death, might not death itself be the final suffering which will purge him completely, the final operation which will restore him to health? If a man is prepared in soul to die, then perhaps any suffering his sins still demand of him will be made up for in the purifying fire of death itself. If he is not at all prepared in soul to die, is he not precisely rejecting God's will for him and choosing that state of alienation from God which we call hell?

This, of course, is a new way of looking at purgatory, but nevertheless does it not satisfy the demands of the Church teaching and the Scriptures quoted in the catechism? The core of this teaching is that the dead need to be prayed for, that they may be released from their sins. But prayer, we must remember, is not only effective in the present and the future, but in the past as well. It can be retrospective. Nothing prevents us from believing that our present prayers and Masses for the dead were of use to them at the hour of their death.

141

THE FORGIVENESS OF SINS

What is the tenth article of the Creed?

The tenth article of the creed is, "the forgiveness of sins."

What is meant by "the forgiveness of sins"?

By "the forgiveness of sins" is meant that Christ has left the power of forgiving sins to the pastors of his Church.

By what means are sins forgiven?

Sins are forgiven principally by means of the sacraments of baptism and penance.

What is sin?

Sin is an offense against God, by any thought, word, deed, or omission against the law of God.

We believe in the Holy Spirit, the Spirit of God breathed forth on us from the cross. Now, as one of the prayers of the Mass in Pentecost week says, the Holy Spirit is the forgiveness of sins; the spirit of the cross is a spirit of compassion which forgives us our sins and has enabled us as Christians to forgive the sins of others. This is what we believe in and what we pledge ourselves to.

But what is sin? Nowadays the word *sin* is a completely religious word. But in biblical times this was not so. The words the Bible uses for "sin" are the ordinary everyday words for offending, injuring, rebelling against people. If a man sinned against God it meant that he did something to God that was like what happened when he offended his neighbor. So perhaps we can get to know what "sin" means by asking ourselves what we do when we offend our neighbor.

Well, first of all, we hurt his feelings, displease him, and make him angry. The Bible uses this way of talking about God too. The Israelites, it says, sinned against God and provoked him to anger. But, of course, this is a way of speaking, for God is not the sort of person who loses his temper, like men.

So we must go deeper. To offend someone is to injure him, to do harm to him. But, as Job says, what harm can our sins do to God? Here is the real problem about sin and redemption: for if sins do not really harm God, why does he insist on punishment, and go to such extraordinary lengths to rescue us from a punishment that it seems silly to have demanded in the first place?

The truth seems to be that we do not really harm God, but we really harm ourselves. Sins are deviations from our true selves, from the selves that God has made us to be. They are acts in which we, so to speak, un-create ourselves. By sinning we offend against God's plan of creation.

The Hebrews thought of this plan as a plan for their history, promised to them in a covenant signed by God and themselves on Mount Sinai. So to sin was to offend against this covenant. It was to go against this covenant, and especially against its first clause, which said that Israel was to worship God alone. Sin was to go astray from this worship and this devotion to God; it was idolatry in all its forms. Every offense against the law of God could be called a sort of idolatry.

The Christian also sees things in this way: but he sees a much greater plan of history in which the whole world is to be united in love with God. Sin is any offense against this plan of love.

St. John puts it this way: God said in the beginning, Let there be light. And he meant: Let all the world be brought to the light of God's truth and the light of God's love. Sin is any transgression of this commandment, any offense against God's truth and love.

Now when we say that God forgives sin, we mean that however man deviates from God's plan, God is willing and ready to accept the deviation and lead man back into the plan. Indeed, from the very beginning God's plan for man was not one which men merely had to accept passively; it was one in which they had to cooperate in the planning.

God did not provide man with a script; he asked him to work out the play as he went along. He made man free, as we say; and this is the glory of man. Nevertheless, man can either use the freedom arrogantly to set up a plan contrary to God's, or he can use it creatively to discover how to make God's plan a reality in his life.

Sin is man being arrogant; but the forgiveness of sin is God's willingness to accept into his plan whatever man has done, if man turns and offers it to him—if man, that is to say, ceases to be arrogant and rebellious and starts to search for God's plan again. Such a turning on man's part (or as we call it, "conversion") will involve him in humiliation and suffering: the suffering of his own pride. Christ came to show men how to live in love and truth even if it meant humiliation and suffering.

So the forgiveness of sins, God's compassion on men, has been revealed to us in Christ; and it is still with us in those sacraments which make Christ's sufferings and humiliations available to us, especially baptism in which we express our willingness to die with Christ, and penance which is a renewal of our baptism that we can make every time we have sinned.

God has now put his compassion into the hands of the Church, so to speak, and assured us that to turn back to the Church will be turning back to him. And the Church means us. It is not just the pastors of the Church who are gifted with the compassion of God. We must all forgive one another, as Christ says. It is this mutual compassion of Christians that is visibly offered to a man in baptism and in penance. It is this mutual compassion which is the Holy Spirit active in the Church.

How many kinds of sin are there?

There are two kinds of sin, original sin and actual sin.

What is original sin?

Original sin is that guilt and stain of sin which we inherit from Adam, who was the origin and head of all mankind.

What was the sin committed by Adam?

The sin committed by Adam was the sin of disobedience when he ate the forbidden fruit.

Because the doctrine of original sin is so connected in our minds with the story of Adam and Eve, we must make clear from the start that it is a New Testament doctrine, not an Old Testament one. Christians have deduced it from the New Testament teaching that Christ is our only way of salvation.

If Christ is the only way of salvation, then without Christ all men must be liable to damnation, and this can only be so if all men are somehow in sin; and this must be true even of men who have not committed *acts* of sin themselves ("actual sins," as the catechism calls them).

It has always been the belief of the Church, for example, that even babies need to be baptized, and yet they have not actually sinned. So there must be another kind of sin, a sin that one incurs simply by being born, a sin that arises not from some act but from one's very origin.

To explain this teaching the Church has gone deeper into the story of Adam and Eve than the Old Testament ever did. In the Old Testament the Adam-story is a kind of expansion to all mankind of what we may call the Jeroboam-story. Jeroboam was a king of Israel who set up idolatrous shrines and thus sinned personally and actually. But the Old Testament also says that by his actual sin Jeroboam "brought sin on all Israel." The destiny of Israel was so bound up with their king, that when he went astray all Israel went astray with him. They were led into an idolatrous situation.

This way of thinking about a nation is very fundamental to the Old Testament. Thus, for example, every nation's destiny is bound up with the person who gave it its name, with its "father," so to speak. Israel has for its father Jacob, to whom God gave the name "Israel"; and the tribes of Judah, Benjamin, and so on had as their fathers the sons of Jacob who bore those names.

In the Adam-story the Old Testament expands this way of thinking to all men. Mankind's father is somebody who is simply called "Man" (for this is what the Hebrew word *Adam* means). The sinfulness of men is then thought of as something "brought on them" by an actual sin of their father, "Man."

Even the Old Testament was not altogether happy with this way of thinking, and so in Ezekiel we read that God will not visit the sins of a father upon his children. Nevertheless, this was the only way of thinking available to Christian tradition when it wished to explain "original" sin.

So the traditional explanation of original sin runs as follows. Man is by nature subject to death and all the evils bound up with death (and this is what the Old Testament means by saying that man was made from dust). But God offered mankind the gift of freedom from death and evil, which was more than his nature could expect (and this is signified by the "tree of life" that God placed in the garden).

F

Because "man" rejected the garden (Adam's sin), he no longer had access to this gift; he fell back into a "state of nature," so to speak. Being in this state was not now just natural, but also a state contrary to God's will and blameworthy.

The blame rests primarily on Adam, who as "father" of mankind has bequeathed to us a sort of existence which, though natural to us, is not the sort God wanted us to have. But all of us, simply by *existing* in this imperfect way, are involved in Adam's sin; just as one might say that if a man commits murder, his will is primarily responsible, but his hands and his whole body are involved in the sin.

Of course, it is here that the whole difficulty of the idea of original sin lies. How can there be a blame resting on us, which is not our personal blame, but Adam's? Is not blame always personal blame? And if our situation is not personally blameworthy, how is it blameworthy at all?

The difficulty arises from thinking of mankind as a collection of totally independent individuals, with totally independent responsibilities. Yet our experience tells us that no society of men is really like that. We are so bound together that we cannot see any situation simply in terms of independent personal responsibilities. For example, in any society in which the social way of life is built up on exploitation and injustice, no one in that society can escape profiting from such exploitation, even when he is not personally responsible for it. Even the reformer in such a society when he makes use of, let us say, the railways and roads which have been built by underpaid labor, will be maintaining his own standard of life at the expense of others. He may personally be totally opposed to such underpayment, personally not guilty of it, and yet, unless he emigrates from such a society, he cannot escape involvement in the injustice.

148

Now if there is some way in which the social life of all mankind is unjust and untrue to the plan of creation, then even a man totally innocent of the action which caused such injustice and untrueness is nevertheless caught in it. For he cannot emigrate from the human race! He has to *exist,* and just by *existing* he is involved in unjust and untrue existence.
in unjust and untrue existence.

This is a direct result of the nature of man. Man is not just an individual, but an individual who can only exist in society. This means that long before he becomes responsible for directing his own life, certain directions have been laid down for him by the society he belongs to. If there is a society which he necessarily belongs to, like mankind, there is no way in which he can escape into pure independence of responsibility.

One must not say: It is unjust of God to punish men for something they did not personally commit. For this is to say: It is unjust of God to make man man, that is, to make a creature who is not an ideally independent free will, but a concrete creature who has to live in and with all the rest of mankind. God, in making a man, made a creature who was not personally in full charge of his own destiny, but who, to a certain extent, was bound into a common destiny in charge of mankind as a whole. If this whole destiny of mankind went wrong, then, by the law of his creation, each member of mankind necessarily suffers.

The fact that God chose to make such a creature had its advantages and disadvantages, so to speak. The fact that God chose, by his grace, to rescue him from all sin, actual and original, has given us the chance to profit from all the advantages, and free ourselves from all the disadvantages.

Such then is the doctrine of original sin. In recent years much attention has been paid again to this doctrine, mainly because science and biblical study have made it more difficult to believe in an actual historical Adam. If there was no Adam, where does original sin come from? As Pope Pius XII has pointed out: If the existence of a universal state of sin (and therefore the universal need of Christ's salvation) implies an historical Adam, then Christians must believe in an historical Adam, because the universal need of salvation is a revealed truth.

But perhaps there *is* another way of understanding this universal state of sin. Suppose the "tree of life" is a symbol for Christ himself, and that God planned to free history from natural death and evil by coming to take part in it himself. Then the rejection of the "tree of life" is nothing else than the attempt made by Christ's crucifiers to cast God out of history. The Adam-story is a prophecy of Calvary.

It does not really matter that this event happened half-way through the world's history rather than at the beginning. A play is ruined not so much by a failure in its first scene as by a failure in its climax scene. Such a failure ruins the play from beginning to end. So it was with the world's history: it was ruined from beginning to end by men's failure at the crucial moment of God's coming. It was ruined on Calvary.

Yet it was also saved on Calvary, because God *accepted* into his plan this very rejection of Christ, and in this way let that very rejection bring into the world an eternal love and an eternal life.

Has all mankind contracted the guilt and stain of original sin?
All men have contracted the guilt and stain of original sin,
except the Blessed Virgin, who, through the merits of her
divine son, was conceived without the least guilt or stain of
original sin.

What is this privilege of the Blessed Virgin called?
This privilege of the Blessed Virgin is called the immaculate
conception.

One of the things which makes us suspicious of the new thinking
in the Church is that it "soft-pedals" our Lady and her privileges.
We are used to non-Catholics questioning her perpetual virginity,
her immaculate conception, her assumption, her position as
mediatrix of all graces. But it distresses us to find Catholics being
non-committal on these points.

To attain a truly Catholic balance here we must try to understand why such questioning and soft-pedalling occur. It is always
connected with the question: Where have such doctrines come
from? The fact that the Pope has defined some of Mary's privileges does not sufficiently answer this question, for no Catholic
believes that the Pope is a *source* of revelation. The source of
revelation is Christ in Scripture and tradition, and a papal definition is no more than a declaration, free from error, that such-
and-such a doctrine is to be found in Scripture and tradition. But
whereabouts in Scripture and tradition?

Apart from the virgin birth itself, none of these privileges can
be proved with a Scripture text. Will it help to look at tradition?

151

Here there are two difficulties. First, what is tradition and what is not? The Church has not always found it easy to decide whether a certain belief really is a tradition or a deviation from tradition. Even in the early Church some people thought all Christians should be circumcised, some did not; some thought infants should be baptized, some did not. Which was the genuine tradition? It should not distress us that the Church has to ask questions like these even in our own day, and tries to decide which beliefs about our Lady are genuine traditions and which are not.

The second difficulty is that a tradition has not necessarily been handed down explicitly from the beginning. Traditions grow. They result from prolonged meditation on revelation, a meditation which gradually makes explicit what at first was only implicit. Sometimes one can locate the century in which a tradition first became explicit. Thus, it does not seem possible to trace the assumption back before the fourth century. As for the immaculate conception, the greatest of the medieval theologians still regarded it as heresy.

It is true that one can trace from the beginning an urge to declare our Lady the holiest of creatures, but always with a proviso, namely, that the more important truth that Christ is the unique source of all holiness must be preserved. Any statement about our Lady that conflicted with Christ's position would be rejected. Any statement that *seemed* to conflict would be hotly argued, and only accepted if, after long meditation, it became clear that there was no conflict.

One consequence of all this is that traditions cannot always be thought of as records of fact stemming from eyewitnesses; they are often more like deductions from the whole attitude of Christ and his Church towards their mother. So it is that the scriptural belief in the virgin birth grew to a belief in Mary's perpetual virginity, despite scriptural references to Christ's "brothers" and "sisters." Gradually, it was realized that "brothers" could have a wider meaning for Jews than it has for us, and that for the bride of God to have had another husband would have been a sort of adultery.

Again, it was gradually seen that someone who can be called "mother of our Saviour" can also be called "mother of salvation" or "mother of grace" (a more traditional and more accurate title than "mediatrix of graces"). Or again, the Church became convinced that the one woman who already enjoyed intimate unity with Christ on this earth could rightly be granted an anticipation in heaven of the intimate unity with Christ which we shall all enjoy at our resurrection.

Where the immaculate conception was concerned, the Church struggled long between her desire to recognize Mary as "full of grace" in the deepest sense, and the more important desire to teach the truth that all men need Christ's salvation from original sin. Only when she saw that the immaculate conception did not deny Mary's need to be saved from original sin, was the Church happy to accept the doctrine. All the doctrine stated was that Mary's preservation from sin took place, not after her birth, but at the very first moment of her existence.

Now this attempt to preserve importances is still going on. It is a perpetual search for balance. The Council has asked us to "remember that in Catholic teaching there exists an order or hierarchy of truths, since they are not all related in the same way to the central core of the Christian faith." If we forget this fact we shall fall into such "heresies" as the one contained in the catechism answer above. For Mary is *not* the only exception to the universal law of original sin. There is a far more important exception: the man Jesus Christ, her son.

What is actual sin?

Actual sin is every sin which we ourselves commit.

How is actual sin divided?

Actual sin is divided into mortal sin and venial sin.

What is mortal sin?

Mortal sin is a grievous offense against God.

Why is it called mortal sin?

It is called mortal sin because it kills the soul and deserves hell.

How does mortal sin kill the soul?

Mortal sin kills the soul by depriving it of sanctifying grace, which is the supernatural life of the soul.

Is it a great evil to fall into mortal sin?

It is the greatest of all evils to fall into mortal sin.

Where will they go who die in mortal sin?

They who die in mortal sin will go to hell for all eternity.

Normally, we Catholics think of sin as venial. The usual kind of sin is venial sin, and mortal sin is distinguished by being particularly grave—a much bigger sin than our usual failings.

Thus we have been taught to recognize mortal sins by looking for characteristics all connected with the bigness of the sin. Mortal sin requires not only knowledge, but full knowledge; not only consent, but full consent; not only sinful matter, but grave matter. If we steal a small amount the sin is venial; if we steal a large amount the sin is mortal. We are also taught that where the sixth commandment is concerned all sins are big; there is no such thing as a small sexual matter.

154

Ordinary Catholics are often quite spontaneously unwilling to believe in the existence of mortal sins. This is not entirely out of fear (though it is true that we all grasp at reasons for disbelieving in anything we fear); but also because we feel that the whole idea of mortal sins and eternal punishment involves us in an un-Christian idea of God.

Recently, many theologians have given support to our unwillingness to believe in mortal sin, by teaching that full knowledge and consent are very rare since everybody is to some extent a psychiatric case, and by teaching that it is impossible to point out any matter that is grave in itself. One must take into account the circumstances.

Now there are many misunderstandings here. We are reacting against something which is not actually the Church's teaching, and if we really understood the Church's teaching on sin we should not need to react in the way we do.

First of all, mortal sin is not just more of a sin than venial sin; it is a different kind of thing altogether. In fact, this should be obvious from the consequences. The difference between total loss of God in hell and the delayed promise of God which is purgatory is not a difference of degree but a difference in kind. Mortal and venial sin must therefore differ not in degree but in kind. Indeed, the tradition of the Church teaches not that mortal sin is a *fuller* kind of sin than venial sin, but that it is the only sin which truly *fulfills* the definition of sin. As we shall see, there is a sense in which venial sin is not "sin" at all.

When we come to talk of full knowledge and full consent and grave matter, the words *full* and *grave* do not refer to a *degree of fullness* in the knowledge and consent. They refer rather to a knowledge which really *fulfills* the definition of knowledge, a consent which really *fulfills* the definition of

F*   155

consent, a sinful matter which really *fulfills* the definition of sinful matter.

The only real criterion of mortal sin—that is, of true sin—is that it is an action excluding genuine love for God or for others or for ourselves. When we say that it requires full knowledge, we do not primarily mean that it requires expert theoretical knowledge of what the rules are: we mean that sin (to be truly sin) cannot arise from simple ignorance, but must arise from a real act of ignoring the truth of conscience speaking in a person. When we say that it requires full consent, we do not mean that in order to sin we must actually will evil as such, but that sin is a real act of indifference to the true good, arising from a desire to pursue what we want to be good. When we say that true sin involves a grave matter, this does not mean that sin must exclude love in some specially "big" way. Any matter which excludes love at all, is already grave. Sin, to be true sin, is concerned with any such matter.

Church tradition does not in fact make an extraordinary difference between the sixth commandment and the fifth or the seventh. *All* the commandments are about grave matters—matters in which we are neglecting love by taking our neighbor's life, or his wife, or his goods.

Actually, in the final analysis we can never be absolutely certain whether something excludes love or not, whether it is mortal or not. But this does not matter, for the important thing to see is that God is always prepared to forgive. God's generosity and love are shown precisely in his willingness to forgive. It is surely because we have forgotten to see God primarily as generous rather than as judge that we have become so afraid of mortal sin. We flee to the false comfort that perhaps mortal sin is impossible, rather than to the true comfort that it is for-givable.

But in fact, the very existence of mortal sin proves God's generosity. It is only because he has given us the gift of being able to love freely, that we are free *not* to love. The Christian God is precisely the God who in his generosity has allowed us the power to sin but is always prepared to forgive.

What is venial sin?

Venial sin is an offense which does not kill the soul, yet displeases God, and often leads to mortal sin.

Why is it called venial sin?

It is called venial sin because it is more easily pardoned than mortal sin.

Venial is a Latin word which one might translate either as "excusable" or as "pardonable." But the latter translation causes difficulties. It sounds as though the Church is teaching that some sins are pardonable, and some are not, whereas it is the message of the Gospel that all sins are pardonable through Jesus Christ.

The catechism tries to solve the difficulty by saying that venial sins are called "pardonable" because they are *more easily* pardonable than mortal sins. We think of something like treading on a person's toe, which he might resent but which he would find more easily pardonable than, say, the mortal insult of spitting in his face. But, as we said before, there is a real difference in *kind* between venial and mortal sin, not just a difference in degree.

We might do better to use the word *excusable,* and say: Some sins are in themselves excusable, some not; but the great message of Christ is that God will pardon even inexcusable sins. Let us give some examples by way of explanation.

First, if one has a mathematical sum to do, there are two kinds of mistake which he can make. On the one hand, he may have no idea at all *how* to do the sum and make a total hash of it because he has forgotten the right method. On the other hand, he may know the method, but make a silly mistake in multiplication and in fact get the wrong answer. Now these are two quite different types of mistake: one is a mistake in principle, the other gets the principles right but makes a mistake in the working-out.

Or a second example. If one is engaged in a pillow fight, he can lose his balance either totally, and then fall off and lose; or alternatively, he may lose his balance only partially and just wobble, and then there is still the possibility of recovery and of finally winning. In a sense, there is a difference in degree between the losses of balance; but there is also a difference in kind because in one case he loses footing altogether and in the other he does not.

Finally, a third example. Break-ups between friends or in a marriage may be minor or major, differing in degree. But sometimes they also differ in kind, for while some leave in existence a thread of love and trust on which reconciliation can be built, others result in a complete loss of trust and leave nothing left to build on. A bit of rebelliousness here and there, one might say, is excusable; but complete indifference to whether one is loved or not, that is inexcusable.

Now all three examples should help us to understand the difference between mortal and venial sin.

Mortal sin is so indifferent to God's love and to love of our neighbor that the very basis of reconciliation is destroyed; balance on the ground of grace is totally lost; we have committed a real sin in principle, so to speak. Venial sin, on the other hand, rebels against love but does not destroy it; it wobbles, but the wobble is recoverable: it is not a sin in principle but a fault in the working-out.

159

Thus in a sense venial sin can be called "excusable" or "recoverable." If it was a man we were offending this might mean that only venial sin was "pardonable," but in fact the marvelous good news of the Gospel is that God pardons even "inexcusable" sins, if we let him. He stoops down again and again to teach us *how* to solve our problems, to give us another chance on the ground of grace, to trust us again in our relation with him.

This is so important. If, in our fear of sin, we fly for comfort to the idea that perhaps it was not *really* a sin, that perhaps it was only venial, excusable, then are we not perhaps despairing of God's pardon and trying to find another way out of our guilt? Our true comfort is that even when it really is a sin, really inexcusable, nevertheless God will pardon it, if we will accept the forgiveness. Someone has said that modern man has lost his sense of forgiveness, but kept his sense of sin; and one cannot help feeling that hoping our sins are excusable, rather than hoping in God's pardon, results from such a misunderstanding.

Of course, there is a sin which Jesus calls unpardonable—the sin against the Holy Spirit. But is not this just the sin of not being willing to accept forgiveness? The Holy Spirit, as one of the prayers of Mass says, *is* the forgiveness of sins. Is not our tendency to minimize our sins, so that we do not need God's love but only his approval, really this "unpardonable" sin of which Jesus speaks?

RESURRECTION AND ETERNAL LIFE

The Holy Spirit is the wind that not only gathers us around Christ in that community of compassion and reconciliation that we call the Church; he is a wind also driving us on after Christ to the Father. He is, so to speak, the wind left in his wake by Christ as he departed to his Father, a wind which is already blowing us to follow him through resurrection to eternal life.

What is the eleventh article of the Creed?
The eleventh article of the Creed is, "the resurrection of the body."
What is meant by "the resurrection of the body"?
By "the resurrection of the body" is meant that we shall all rise again with the same bodies at the day of judgment.

The immediate question we ask ourselves is: What is the point of the resurrection of the body? Of what use will our bodies be to us in heaven? If we are thinking of our bodies simply as instruments or tools that we make use of in this world in order to get to the next, then this question is a good question. The man who has been using a spade to dig himself out of a prison camp throws the spade away when he reaches freedom; he has no more use for it.

But this is a mistaken way of looking at things. We must not think of ourselves merely as individual souls, or of heaven simply as that eternal joy which fills each individual soul when it gets out of purgatory. For God is not thinking only of individual souls, but of his whole creation. What he is working towards is a renewal of the whole of creation, the coming of "a new heaven and a new earth," as the New Testament puts it.

The whole world, as St. Paul tells us, is subject to frustration, death, and decay, and this was not meant by God. We feel it in ecstatically happy moments when we cry out, "Oh, if only this moment could last forever!" And yet it has to pass, to decay, to be lost apparently forever. But St. Paul goes on to tell us that God is going to free the whole world from this bondage to decay, and that he will do so when "the sons of God" are made manifest, when mankind rises to eternal life.

So, to begin with, the resurrection of the body means much more than the resurrection of our individual bodies; it means the resurrection of the whole world. That is why it has to wait until the world is completed. If it was only a matter of our individual bodies, God could raise them as soon as we die; but the resurrection of our bodies is only part of a general resurrection of the whole world, and this must wait till the whole world dies.

Perhaps we should understand all this better if we thought of our bodies as musical instruments by means of which God wishes us to produce fine melodies in this world, melodies meant to last forever; or better still, if we thought of our bodies as the outward sound of those melodies, and our souls as their inward structure. At the moment, we are very imperfectly present to what we are doing with our bodies, and cannot grasp the melody very clearly. But God is even now, in eternity, present fully to the melody we are playing, and not only to our melody but to the melodies of the whole world, from its beginning to its end.

We from our standpoint hear the world as a terrible cacophony; but he from his standpoint hears it as a perfect, harmonious symphony of sound.

Now to go to heaven means to join God where he is, and so it will include being present to the world that we once lived in and the bodies we once were, but being present to them as he now is. Part of heaven will be being present again to this world we live in, but now enjoyed forever as a perfect symphony of sound. That is what is meant by the world being renewed, brought to life again, resurrected; and part of the resurrection of the world will be the resurrection of our own particular thread of melody as part of the whole, our own life renewed and living forever in its true context.

But, of course, this can only happen when the world is complete—at the last day, as we say. Heaven *before* this time is not the full heaven that God intends; it is a heaven waiting for the concert to begin, so to speak. Only on the last day will the whole world be complete.

Yet, in a way, the resurrection is already in progress, because the main theme of the concert has already been determined— Christ's life. We on earth are all trying to learn this theme and accompany it in our own way. The music has already started though we cannot hear it very well; but God can hear it, and it is because of the theme of his Son running through it that it is harmonious to him. Into that music we shall enter on the last day. That is what is meant by saying that Christ has already risen from the dead; and that we live now, not ourselves, but Christ in us. The sacraments, for example, are even now communicating the melody of Christ's risen life to us; and especially is this true of the sacrament of the Eucharist in which our bodies are already touched and transformed by his risen body. All this is the beginning here on earth of the resurrection of the body; for as our Lord himself said, "Anyone who eats my flesh and drinks my blood *has eternal life,* and I shall raise him up on the last day."

So the resurrection of the body will be an entry into God's presence in Christ to this universe in which we are living now. The bodies we shall have in the risen world are the bodies we are living in now, but our presence to them will be new: for, as St. Paul says, the present perishable nature will have put on imperishability, and this mortal nature will have put on immortality.

What is the twelfth article of the Creed?

The twelfth article of the Creed is, "life everlasting."

What does "life everlasting" mean?

"Life everlasting" means that the good will live forever in the glory and happiness of heaven.

What is the glory and happiness of heaven?

The glory and happiness of heaven is to see, love, and enjoy God forever.

What does Scripture say of the happiness of heaven?

Scripture says of the happiness of heaven that "eye has not seen nor ear heard, neither has it entered into the heart of man, what things God has prepared for them that love him."

Everlasting life can have at least three different meanings.

The life we live now continually moves forward from one moment to another, from the present into the future. Everlasting life might be thought of as such a moving life going on forever. If this picture were correct, heaven would be a perpetual moving forward into an infinite future. The difficulty about this description of heaven is that every move forward is a loss as well as a gain; we lose the present moment in order to gain the future moment. Everlasting life so conceived would be a process of infinite loss just as much as it would be a process of infinite gain.

There is another kind of everlastingness: the everlastingness of such truths as two plus two equal four. Because these truths do not change at all from moment to moment they lose nothing from moment to moment, but then they do not gain anything either; in fact, they are not alive at all. Their everlastingness is not an everlasting life.

If we are to get a true picture of everlasting life we must take a part of each of the above meanings and weave them together. Everlasting life will then not be a perpetual process of passing from one joyful moment to another, nor a sort of total stillness and unchangingness completely abstracted from life, but the simultaneous presence of all the joys of life together in one and the same joy.

We have to fight here against the notion that that much life can hardly be gotten into one moment, for in this world we can only get so much life and no more into any moment. If we are to experience a real fullness of life, we think, we will have to add moment to moment in a long line and pass through them one by one. But this is not the only way to add one moment of life to another. Moments can be added one on top of another, not one moment *after* another. And indeed we often do this (at least partially) when, living in one moment, we remember or anticipate another moment. But God does this totally. All the moments of his life are enjoyed together in their fullness. Such a life is more alive than our perpetual hurrying forward into the future.

Perhaps we will understand all this better if we reflect that a certain coalescence of time always accompanies deep joy, even in this world. When we really taste joy in this world, we do not notice the passing of time; the moments we are living through seem to coalesce together into one big experience. Joy is characterized not by extremely busy movement from one moment to another, but by a sort of tremendous stillness which enters into our outward activity from inside, and produces in us a sort of ecstasy. The way in which we should conceive of heaven is as an absolutely total and infinite ecstasy in which all the moments of history will coalesce into a deep stillness of delight. This indeed is the way God is present to the whole world and enjoys the whole of history. Heaven is to share in God's everlasting life.

At this point we should realize that the important word in the phrase "life everlasting" is the first word, *life,* and not the second one, *everlasting.* We should not think that we already know what life means from our experience of it here and now, and that all that will happen in heaven is that we shall gain it forever. Compared with God's life in heaven, what we have now is a sort of death, and if it were to go on forever we should really be more justified in calling it "everlasting death" than "everlasting life." What God has promised us in heaven is the true life which gathers up all the joy that can be reaped from every moment of human existence, every moment of the world's history, and gathers it into one tremendous moment of eternal joy.

Yet a second point emerges. Everlasting life is a name for God himself, for the life of God; and of this life we *do* have a kind of experience even on earth. We do not have to wait for everlasting life until after death, it has already penetrated into our life now. Because we are Christians we are given a capacity for greater joy in the world than have people who are not gifted with the revelation that comes through Christ. In our faith we can believe that evil is overcome, that sin cannot finally conquer, that, as St. Paul says, "everything in this world works together for our good." In our faith we can see that we are infinitely loved, loved by God, loved by his universe. This vision, granted to us through faith, can bring us even now some taste of the eternal joy that is stored up for us. Everlasting life begins upon this earth.

And so, although the merely human eye has not seen and the merely human ear has not heard, still, something of what God has stored up for us does enter into the Christian heart of man, and this more and more as we learn to recognize his presence in our life here and now.

Shall not the wicked also live forever?

The wicked also shall live and be punished forever in the fire of hell.

We have an odd example here of how a word can mean two different things; and not only two different things, but two diametrically opposed things. For even if the wicked "live forever" they do not enter into "eternal life." "Eternal life" is another name for heaven, another name for God. To enter into eternal life is to go to heaven. This is exactly what the wicked do not do. They enter into eternal death.

It is for this reason that the Scriptures do not use the phrase "live forever" about the wicked, but only about the saints in heaven. Whatever "life" the wicked have after the judgment is not, according to the Scriptures, to be dignified with the name of "life" at all. So we find it written: "Those who did good will rise again to life; and those who did evil, to condemnation." Or again: "The wicked will go away to eternal punishment, and the virtuous to eternal life."

In order to understand the scriptural way of looking at things, we must remember that there are two different meanings of the word *hell* in the Bible. In the Old Testament, "hell" translates the Hebrew word *sheol,* which was nothing but a poetical way of talking about Death itself. Sheol is a pit that swallows one up, a bottomless grave without exit, a place of darkness and silence, dust and oblivion, the sheer dead-end of life. This idea passes through into the New Testament, too, where the Greek word *hades* is used. But in the New Testament this hell is no longer a place without escape, for Christ has risen from the dead. "He was not abandoned to hades, nor did his flesh see corruption."

However, the New Testament also teaches that Christ's resurrection is the *only* escape from death, so that the people who reject Christ, and therefore cannot avail themselves of the power of his resurrection, seal themselves into *sheol* in a new and terrible way. Life has been offered to them in Christ, but they choose rather an eternal death from which there can be no further escape. For this new death the New Testament has a new word. This word is *gehenna* (also translated as "hell" in the *New English Bible*) and it derives from a place outside Jerusalem, the valley of Gehenna or the valley of the sons of Hinnom, which had already become in the Old Testament a symbol for God's wrath and for the judgment that was to come upon the world. As far as we can make out, this valley had originally been the site of a pagan shrine, in which human sacrifice was offered to the god Moloch and burnt with fire. The shrine itself was called Topheth, which may mean "fireplace."

Thus Isaiah already prophesied the day of judgment in these terms:

> *See the name of Yahweh coming from afar, blazing in his anger. . . . His lips brim with fury, his tongue is like a devouring fire, his breath is like a river in spate. . . .*

> *He will make his majestic voice to be heard, and display his arm falling to strike, in the ferocity of his anger, in the glare of a devouring fire, in cloudburst, downpour and hailstones. . . .*

> *For in Topheth there has been prepared for Moloch a pit deep and wide with fire and wood in plenty.*

The breath of Yahweh like a stream of brimstone will set fire to it.

Here we can see the beginnings of our Christian symbols for hell. The burning fire of Gehenna is the Old Testament fire of judgment. Thus when the New Testament says that some people will not see the resurrection to life but only a resurrection to judgment, when it says that some people are cut off from the one escape from death and will therefore be plunged into a "second death," it is small wonder that it pictures this state of death under the images of devouring fire.

Furthermore, this fire is eternal, at least in the sense that there is no coming back out of it, no redemption from it. For it symbolizes the final rejection of Christ; and since Christ is the only redemption, anyone who has finally rejected him has finally rejected redemption.

Whether this fate also implies that the fire is something which lasts on and on forever never-endingly seems to be still open to theological discussion. In the Old Testament, "fire" symbolized total destruction, from which there was obviously no return; and when the Church teaches the eternity of hell, she is rejecting a notion of hell as temporary suffering followed by a new redemption. Hell is eternal because it is the road of no return, of no eventual redemption.

CONCLUSION

The Creed is our Christian proclamation of God's faithful love for us, and our oath of fealty to him. It tells the story of what God is doing in the universe and promises our cooperation and fidelity.

We might summarize the story of what God is doing in the universe with the help of the old story of Pygmalion, the sculptor who carved a statue with whom he fell in love. The statue came to life and returned his love. Now God has brought this universe into existence out of love for it, and in mankind this universe has come to life, so to speak; the universe is able to answer God in love through the creature man. This is a Christian way of talking about the process of evolution in which the universe in response to God's creative Spirit has finally produced man, a creature who no longer responds to God simply by being but also by loving.

However, there is a second level to this story. God has not only produced mankind (the creation through which the universe can speak to God), but he has produced within mankind Jesus Christ (through whom mankind is enabled to speak to God as to a Father). In Jesus Christ mankind itself attained a new level of life, the life of God himself—men are given the gift of loving God with the same strength and intensity with which they are loved, loving God as a Son loves his Father.

It is this story that the Creed tells. It tells us how Jesus Christ—in the moments of his passion, death, and resurrection—was dis-

172

playing his love for his Father, returning the love with which the Father had given him birth, going back to the Father from whom he had come. The life with which he is alive is the life of God himself, the Spirit of God, the breath or wind of God. That breath or wind is now also alive in us, left behind, so to speak, as the wind left by Christ's passing to his Father. We are gathered up by that wind, inspired by that breath, and carried ourselves towards the Father with the very life of God in us. We too are to pass through passion, death, and resurrection, the Sonship of God is to become fully alive in us, and we are destined for eternal life in our Father's house.

In the Creed we promise our cooperation with this creation of God. Here in the world, inspired by the wind of Christ's passing, we are formed into a Church, reconciled to God by forgiveness of sins. We follow the leadership of Jesus, born, suffering, dying, being raised and taken up to God's right hand. We too are to go by way of resurrection to God's right hand, where we shall meet the Son at his second coming, and be taken to the Father, taken into eternal life. This is the Christian belief expressed in the words of the Apostles' Creed:

I believe in God, the Father almighty, creator of heaven and earth; and in Jesus Christ, his only Son, our Lord, who was conceived by the Holy Spirit, born of the virgin Mary, suffered under Pontius Pilate, was crucified, died, and was buried. He descended into hell; the third day he rose again from the dead; he ascended into heaven, and sits at the right hand of God, the Father almighty, from thence he shall come to judge the living and the dead. I believe in the Holy Spirit, the holy catholic Church, the communion of saints, the forgiveness of sins, the resurrection of the body, and life everlasting.

Amen.